The Promise
I Kept

My Journey With Dad
From Home Care Through Hospice

JACKIE MADDEN HAUGH

Virginia

Published in the United States by WriteLife Publishing
(An imprint of Boutique of Quality Books Publishing Company)
www.writelife.com

Printed in the United States of America
978-1-60808-187-5 (p)
978-1-60808-188-2 (e)

Library of Congress Control Number: 2018930303

Book design by Robin Krauss, www.lindendesign.biz
Cover design by Marla Thompson, www.edgeofwater.com

First editor: Olivia Swenson
Second editor: Pearlie Tan

PRAISE FOR
JACKIE MADDEN HAUGH
AND

The Promise I Kept

"For every person who has ever made a promise to a loved one and struggled to keep it, to all who have ushered a soul from life to death, to those who aren't sure how to manage and support an aging parent, this book is for you. Jackie brilliantly and with humor invites you to walk with her through the struggle and triumphs of the parent child relationship, when roles are reversed and the adult child must take charge. She challenges her reader to look at death and dying through the lens of life and living and in doing so replaces fear with love."

— Sheila Ellison,
Author and Founder of Single Moms Connect

This book is dedicated to those who have sacrificed much to care for a loved one. It is a thankless job and one we're typically unprepared for, but with your divine spirit shining brightly, you have showed compassion, patience, and love to a soul in their greatest time of need.

Acknowledgments

Our life stories are never written alone. There is always a host of people who have led us along the way, intentionally or not, to where we were meant to go. This story could never have happened without the support, patience, and blessed love I received from so many, and I would be remiss if I did not mention them here.

First, to my brothers David and Tim Madden. While geography made it difficult for them to be with me all the time, I always knew they were just a phone call away, especially if I needed them to talk me off the ledge I occasionally found myself dangling from. And, when I truly needed their physical help, they dropped everything without question to be by my side.

Next, I'd like to thank caregivers Enemi Helu, Emori Suevdre, and Mike Toll. Without their kindness, support, and help, I could have never taken on this carer role. While their job was to attend for my father's physical needs, I often found them nurturing my emotional ones.

To the "Daddy Sitters," Kelly Cheek, Elizabeth Cook, and Cassie O'Hearn—bless you. When he was awake, you sat with him and talked or sang to him. You helped Dad feel like he was still a viable human being and alive.

Then, there were the two beautiful women who brought my father Communion every Sunday: Kelly Cook and Sue Marion.

Receiving the sacrament was the most important part of Dad's week—it was a ritual he honored and treasured. And, to Father Warrick James, our Pastor at St. Simon Church, who calmed Dad's fears about the end of life's journey. Sitting with him on a regular basis, together they discussed theology and the sins he felt he committed over his lifetime. With Father Warrick's absolution and blessing, Dad was able to make complete peace with his life.

To my mentor, writing coach, and dear friend, Sheila Ellison: without you, I never would have had the courage to put my thoughts onto paper. You guided me to write without fear, free and open.

And, finally, to my four children: Michelle, Jenni, Lauren, and Timmy. We started our journey when I was the mom who took care of you. But as you grew into adults and my life became complicated, you stepped in to take care of me. You lifted me off the ground when I fell. You dried my tears and supported all my decisions, even when they greatly affected you. And, with your love, you allowed me to give your grandfather a dignified and peaceful passing. For that, I'm eternally grateful.

INTRODUCTION

My Special Man

Standing in a long line at Starbucks one dreary November morning in 2016, I did what I usually do to kill time while waiting for my double cappuccino—I asked the woman in front of me about her life. As a writer, I'm always curious about what makes others tick, for we all have a unique story that belongs to us and us alone. But before I could drill deep and unpeel the layers of her world, she turned the conversation around to me.

"Don't you write for the *Los Altos Town Crier*?" she asked, recognizing my face from the picture beside my column.

"Yes, I do!" I exclaimed, delighted to meet a reader. "I've been submitting stories since 2010."

"I thought that was you. I read it every month," she told me with a bright smile.

I beamed. "Why, thank you!"

Before I knew it, we were discussing some of the topics I wrote about, my first published book, *My Life in a Tutu*, and my current project, *The Promise I Kept*.

"I don't know how writers do it," my new friend said as we moved two steps closer to our coffee. "I can't even write a letter."

Having heard this a million times, I told her my skill hadn't arrived until after my kids were grown up and my husband and I divorced. In high school and college, a learning disability that went undiagnosed in my youth made reading and comprehending a complete nightmare for me. Unless it was some racy novel or a murder mystery, the words just dissipated into the space between the page and my eyes without ever connecting with my brain.

"We never know what hidden talents we own until the timing is right to give birth to them," I answered, patting her shoulder to reassure her that she too could write—or do whatever else she wanted.

After a few other questions, she moved onto the topic of my father. I'd written several articles for the newspaper about our time together before he passed away and the caregiving process for an aging parent.

"How many years did you take care of him?"

Remembering as if it were yesterday, I grinned. "Nine years. After my mother died in 2003, it became his turn to have someone look after him. He was alone, crippled, and slowly losing his eyesight."

We talked about the complexities of being a caregiver: the time lost for personal endeavors, the depletion of finances, and the boredom. Oh, the boredom. But also, when all was said and done, the great rewards.

Just before grabbing her cup, she turned to me and said with a smile, "If you're writing a book about him, he must have been very special. I don't think I'd have that much to say about my father."

Looking into her warm brown eyes and sensing her question about what made my father special, I wondered, how do I explain the relationship between an extroverted daughter who loves parties, dancing, and talking to everyone, and her introverted father, who lived most of his life in his head?

To many, Dad might have appeared ordinary. He didn't invent anything that made a mark on the world—no cure for cancer, no walks on the moon, nothing to ease the burden of the working man. Dad's life was order, routine, and work—lots of work. If he wasn't at his job in San Francisco, he was home cleaning toilets, washing windows, mowing the grass, and pulling weeds. He wasn't a mover or a shaker—parties often left him exhausted, and he rarely belly laughed.

What he was, however, was solid, trustworthy, and devoted to his faith. He was always ready to help anyone who needed it. When we were on a family picnic at Half Moon Bay in 1960, he rescued a drunk man caught in the raging surf—and my father didn't even know how to swim. He was a man who applauded our accomplishments but never took them on as his own. Our personal successes and who we became as adults didn't define who he was as a father or man because he was confident in who he was. He showered us in unconditional love, a phrase often bandied about, but true for him. No matter what we did or how we acted, we always knew he loved us deeply.

The most common description I heard from anyone who took the time to get to know him was, "Your father is such a good, kind man." Such characteristics are rare in our fast-paced society of entitled "me first" Silicon Valley dwellers.

In 1916, John Joseph Madden (better known as Jack), a stoic Irish Catholic, was born to immigrant parents and groomed from an early age to never show emotion. To cry or appear weak was unmanly. Typical of his generation, Dad focused on his duty to his family, rather than connecting with his children.

It was his role to earn money to keep our home fires burning while our mother tended to the child rearing, discipline, and conversation. My father was not only the strong type, but often deathly silent.

In my youth, I accepted that this was who he was even though I craved to know him on a more personal level. How I would have loved to have him more present in my life—to take me to the park, tell me stories, and play house with me. Each night as he sat in his recliner after a wordless dinner, pipe and newspaper in hand, I often found myself wondering, what do you think about? Despite the fact that he appeared emotionally vacant much of the time, I never doubted he loved me by the look in his eyes whenever I entered the room.

Just before I left for college, I decided it was time to learn more about the man who helped my mother bring me into the world.

"Dad, talk to me! I know nothing about you," I implored one night as we sat outside having dinner together. It was a blistering hot July evening in 1971 and I was about to embark on my college career at the University of San Francisco. My mother and brothers were out for the evening, and I was left to act as the lady of the house—responsible for turning on the oven and heating up our Swanson's TV dinners.

Staring at his meal, which he wanted to inhale before it became cold, my father sighed. Dinnertime interruptions were never welcome, but he apparently knew from the intense look in my eyes that I was not about to be deterred from getting what I wanted.

Putting down his fork, he wiped his mouth with a paper napkin, folded his hands on the table, and asked, "What do you want to know?"

"Everything!"

For the next hour, I learned the bullet points of his life: He had grown up poor in San Francisco during the Great Depression, which made life nearly impossible. He took higher education at St. Mary's College in Moraga, California, and held two jobs as a bus boy to pay for his tuition. Then we hit a roadblock. Most men of the Greatest Generation went to war but never talked of it. He had served in World War II but clearly didn't want to go into any detail. There was no depth to his story, no emotion—only the facts.

After heating up his dinner again, I let him get on with his meal, but not before asking, somewhat confused, "Dad, why haven't you told me any of this before? I've heard all of Mom's stories a million times."

Picking up his fork and laying the napkin in his lap, he looked up. "No one ever asked me."

It was the turning point for future discussions, the most poignant of which came in his later years. In 2003, a promise I'd made to him thirteen years before was called in. For the next nine years, life became about Dad and me as we cared for one another—me for his physical needs, him for my spiritual ones. It was during those vulnerable times that I learned who my father really was.

My father was a simple man who believed in the art of surrender when life became challenging. By living with a grateful heart, he carried a happy heart. My father walked daily with his deep connection to the Lord and all of life's possibilities.

My father was also pure love and constantly taught me to honor the souls of humanity, not their physicality. He'd say, "Some people are hard to be around. Human falseness and ego can do that, but it's the soul God sees and loves, so learn to love that in everyone."

In between the boredom and diapers, my father's strength, honesty, gentle and optimistic nature made me pause and revisit how I was living my own life—a life that perhaps needed some adjustment.

Smelling my freshly brewed coffee, I looked at the woman with inquisitive eyes standing in front of me, and was brought back to the moment. Grabbing my cappuccino, I shook her hand, thanked her for the conversation, and just as we turned to go our separate ways, I answered, "Yes, he was truly special and his story needs to be told."

CHAPTER 1

Promises Should Never Be Broken

The mantra "promises made should never be broken" sat on the top rung of my parents' moral ladder, alongside no cheating, lying, or dishonoring the family name with inappropriate behavior in public. Being a "good girl" in the 1950s and 60s, these promises were easy to keep. But, as I tiptoed into my teenage years, others became just too hard.

In 1968, I was in my sophomore year at Mercy High in Burlingame, an all girl's Catholic school. While the blue and white uniforms made us look like a sea of Smurfettes, I found ways to set myself apart from the throng. It was the era of long hair, typically straightened with an iron and ironing board, but mine was worn in a shoulder-length flip. Throwing on a navy-blue vest and brown-and-tan shoes (a big no-no when cardigan sweaters with pearl buttons and white shoes were required as part of the uniform), I could at least be myself on the long bus ride. But the minute I stepped onto campus, out came the prescribed apparel hidden in my backpack, and my signature look was locked away until school was dismissed.

While I was forced to conform, never did I want to appear like everyone else, even when white go-go boots and John

Lennon hats were the rage. Instead, I leaned toward my hippie nature with handmade clothes that I covered in embroidered flowers and hearts.

Each morning, staring at the reflection in my bedroom vanity mirror, I'd smooth the few frizzy strands of hair with a little spit, double check my mascara and eyeliner to be sure none had drifted south to my pink cheeks, and look at my teeth one last time for any remnants of breakfast my toothbrush had missed. While I wasn't trying to impress the other girls with my budding beauty, I just never knew when a cute boy might cross my path.

One particular morning, my mother's voice interrupted my regular beauty ritual. "Jackie, I need your help getting dinner ready tonight," Mom called from the kitchen. "I'll be late and you know how your dad wants his meal the moment he walks in the door."

While Lassie Pearce Madden may have appeared to be "just" a housewife, there was nothing ordinary about her. The daughter of silent movie actors during the reign of W. D. Griffith in the early 1900s, everything she said or did had a flair of the dramatic. She was a woman ahead of her time: she had a high-powered job at Standard Oil in San Francisco just before World War II and drove a car when other women depended on the men in their lives to get around. My mother was beautiful, funny, and well-read, with defined opinions on how life should unfold (often not agreeing with my dad's). Her magnetic personality lit up any room she entered. She was a force to be reckoned with.

Applying one last layer of gloss to accentuate my sixteen-year-old pout, I mumbled a reply under my breath, "Yeah, yeah."

"All you have to do is take the casserole out of the freezer when you get home. You have a half-day today, right?" she went on. "Then, stick it in the oven at 400 degrees. Do it at five."

Hmm, maybe a little more eyeliner is in order too. I smeared on an extra swipe of Cover Girl midnight blue for good measure.

"Jackie, I didn't hear you. Are you listening to me?"

Throwing my burdensome backpack filled with thick history and chemistry books across my shoulder, I pulled a knitted ski cap over my ears to drown out the nagging sound of her voice.

"Yeah, Mom, I heard you."

"Promise me you'll do this."

Holy crap! Shut up!

"Jackie?"

"Okay, okay, Mom. I promise."

"Be sure you do it. I'm counting on you."

While my studies as a sophomore were important, it was extracurricular activities that took up most of my free time. Neil Armstrong was walking on the moon and exploring the beyond, but I was conquering my own planet: dating. There were plans to be made—how to snag the latest flavor of the month, what outfit to wear so he'd sit up and notice, and ways to style my hair and makeup to be truly picture-perfect at any given moment.

And, if the phone magically ring-a-dinged with a possible date for Friday night, any thought of a past promise scattered like leaves on a windy fall day, especially any promises regarding the Tuesday night special, tuna casserole.

Arriving home at lunchtime, I first became distracted with The Phil Donahue Show, figuring I had plenty of time, when a call came from the captain of the Serra High School football team, the all boys' version of my high school. Before I knew it, it was 5:30 p.m.

"Shit!" I screamed, jumping off my parents' bed. "Bob, I've gotta go. I have to put dinner in the oven."

Slamming down the rotary phone and racing to the kitchen, I grabbed Mom's favorite easy-bake pan of chicken of the sea, complete with canned peas and carrots smothered in some pre-fabricated thick cream sauce. Next, I cranked the oven into overdrive, setting the temperature at 650 degrees.

I tossed a salad with limp butter lettuce, cherry tomatoes, and a few dried-up croutons and drowned it in my dad's favorite Bernstein's Italian dressing.

The final chore was setting the table. Instead of my normal willy-nilly way, I took extra care to place the utensils in their "Miss Manners" correct spot, with forks on the left and spoons and knives on the right. Finally, to top off the look, I added fresh flowers from Mom's garden.

"Whew!" I muttered, running to the couch to read my new issue of Seventeen magazine.

Five minutes later, in walked my mother.

"Oh, honey," she chirped, eyeing the table. "Everything looks beautiful. Thank you so much."

Soon after, the head of our household, our hardworking father, came through the front door at six o'clock on the dot.

"Call your brothers. I'll take it from here."

Gathering around the table, the evening ritual began with bowed heads and grace. Sucking in air, my silent prayer to the heavens above pleaded that all would be right in cuisine land. But, as my luck would have it, Julia Childs I was not.

"This is frozen!" Dad uttered in surprise with a mouthful of icy sludge. Spitting the casserole back onto his yellow plastic plate, he looked questioningly in my mother's direction.

"What?" Mom uttered, shock appearing on her unsuspecting face. Stabbing her fork into the thawed mushy coating, her utensil hit an iceberg. Turning her laser eyes in my direction, she demanded, "What time did you put this in the oven?"

"Five, just like you told me to."

"Are you lying to me?"

Caught in the 11th commandment, "Thou shalt not lie to Lassie," I broke down and sobbed.

"I'm sorry. I was on the phone and time just got away. I wasn't paying attention and . . ."

"I don't want to hear any more. Go to your room."

Normally, escaping to my room meant refuge from the constant noise made by my three brothers. But when mom sent me there, death felt like a better alternative.

"Jackie, do you know how disappointed I am with you?" Mom hissed as she ushered me out of the kitchen and stood in the doorway to my room. "You promised!"

"I'm sorry."

"You broke your word," she said in frustration. "Next time, don't promise something if you can't deliver."

Never wanting to hurt my mother, I broke down in tears over the selfishness of my youth. It was in that moment I made a pledge to myself and the universe: there'd never be a next time. If I uttered the words "I promise," I'd follow through, no matter how difficult the task. After all, people depended on me.

It wasn't until years later that my commitment to keeping my promises was truly tested. In 1981, my ninety-two-year-old maternal grandmother Helen came to live with my parents.

She'd been having fainting spells and the doctor said she could no longer live alone. It was just the beginning of health issues popping up in my family.

Ironically, my mother had constantly told me and my brothers that when the time came, she and Dad wanted to be put in a home—the last thing they wanted was to inconvenience their children. But when it came to Lassie caring for her mother, that was a different story. Despite the fact that Mom was beginning her spiral into the world of poor health with breast cancer, degenerative back issues, and rheumatoid arthritis, she took Helen in. And, with help from my father and us kids from time to time, they managed.

But in 1984, at the age of sixty-eight, my father suffered a debilitating stroke, leaving him weakened with minimal use of his left leg. His left arm was completely dead. As time wove in circles around the sun, mobility became more challenging and so too, his ability to help my mother around the house.

For the next six years, the three of them struggled to get through their days until lifting my grandmother from her bed to her wheelchair proved to be an impossible task. Home care was not a popular idea in the 1980s, so the only solution, as my parents saw it, was putting Helen in a nursing home where she'd be cared for.

One sunny spring afternoon in March 1990, shortly after my mom had settled Grammy into "the facility," I took my father for a visit. He adored his mother-in-law and missed her.

Laboriously making his way up the wheelchair ramp, I fully grasped how debilitated he had become. Instead of the agile, speed-walking man who trekked miles each morning to get to early Mass at our parish, St. Charles, he looked like a tattered, weather-beaten scarecrow. With one strong gust of wind from the northeast, I was sure he'd fall over.

Resting between each step, his left arm dangling at his side like a broken pendulum in a grandfather clock, I witnessed his internal battery slowly running out of steam, and my eyes began to sting. Children, no matter how old we become, are never prepared to watch our parents age.

But as he teetered up the ramp inch by inch, I found myself becoming antsy. I didn't have all day. While my children were safe and waiting for me at home with a babysitter, as far as I saw it, only I could attend to their every need perfectly. Only I could make peanut butter and jelly sandwiches just the way they liked them. I needed to get home.

Hoping to diffuse my building impatience, I asked, "Dad, isn't it a beautiful day?"

"What did you say?"

"The weather, Dad. Isn't it a nice day?"

No response.

Shading my eyes from the glare of the midday sun with the back of my hand, I scanned the unkempt grounds. I was grateful my horticulturist grandmother had lost her sight long ago as this would have made her terribly unhappy. Her spirit would have died right alongside the wasted garden.

While it was spring and the rest of the world was coming back to life, apparently the facility hadn't gotten the memo. A once-prolific rose garden sat petrified. Black buds dangled from long fossilized stalks that hadn't had a proper pruning in years. Thin stems of impatiens, which when in full bloom served as a well-tailored honor guard along the walkway for residents, were now leggy and flaccid, in desperate need of a prescription of Viagra for flowers. Off to the right, a grove of gnarly, lifeless orange trees sat silhouetted against the faded pink wall of the building. Decorated with only a few shriveled orange balls, the dead branches cried out for a good Texas chainsaw massacre.

"How are you doing, Dad?" I checked in as he took another painful step.

"This place is so ugly," he breathed heavily, his brow now glistening with perspiration. "I don't know why your mom thought this was a good idea."

Sadly, I couldn't agree more. While the grounds were bad enough, the building was worse.

Built in the 1940s, the facade didn't just need some lipstick and rouge; it needed a complete Hollywood facelift. Faded flesh-colored paint peeled away from the cracked stucco as spider web fissures wove a labyrinth in several of the single-paned windows. On those windows were rusty bars. Was it to keep intruders out or the inmates from escaping?

"So, Dad? How about those 49ers?" I tried once more, hoping to keep his gaze away from the broken-down surroundings. "That was some game last night, huh?"

His six-foot-tall body seemed to be morphing into that of an ostrich with his head bowed low as if looking for a nice soft pile of sand to hide in. He was now bent completely in half, struggling to follow my conversation and continue walking.

"I'm sorry, honey. You keep talking, but I can't hear you."

As he rubbed his ear, I wondered if wax build-up had clogged his ear canal.

"Never mind." I sighed, gently brushing the palm of my hand up and down his crooked spine. "We're almost there. How are you doing?"

Carefully manipulating his cane for added assurance and balance, he was one step from the top.

"I don't like this place," he mumbled.

"I know. I don't either, but Gram is safe here."

Just as I stepped between my father and the battered front door to enter the facility, his body began to shake wildly.

"Dad," I cried, grasping his shoulders. "Are you okay?"

If I didn't know better, I would have thought he was having an epileptic attack as I watched his one good arm fly in the air searching to retain his balance.

"My cane! Oh, God. Where's my cane?" he cried as it went flying.

"Stand right here, don't move. Hold the rail tight." Molding his gnarled fingers around the oxidized banister, I wished they made crazy glue for human skin. "I'll go get it."

Scrambling to retrieve his lifeline to his physical world, I was shocked that not one member of the staff had emerged to respond to his cries. Was everyone in white taking a nap with his or her elderly charges? Shouldn't there be screens or monitors to witness the comings and goings of the residents and their aging guests?

"Where the hell is help when you need it?" I hissed loud enough to send the robins pecking the dirt to a higher perch.

Racing back just in time, I wrapped my arms around his wavering frame. Hugging him with every ounce of strength I had, I shook, terrified I might lose him over the edge.

"Here, Dad. Here's your cane," I whispered, kissing him on the cheek and placing his cane back in his one good hand.

While sweat ran in rivulets through the canyons deeply

imbedded on his seventy-four-year-old face, he regained his composure long enough to say, "Thank you, honey."

Then, like a bomb exploding, it happened. The grenade of his greatest fear was thrown in my face.

"Jackie, promise me you'll never do this to me. Please!"

"What?"

"Promise me you'll never put me in a home," he cried again. "I don't want to live like this."

For a moment, the world fell off its axis. What happened to my parents' earlier insistence about putting them in a home when the time came and not wanting to be a bother? Then I remembered. It was only my mother who had ever said those words. True to his nature, Dad sat quietly devouring his dinner as she made plans for both of their futures.

Cupping both my hands around the gentle face of the man I called Daddy, I knew in that divine moment what I was being called to do.

Taking out the imaginary gold pen I kept for the forever vows—like my marriage, loving my children until the day I died, and living a life of faith—I held my dad like I'd never held him before and declared, "I promise, Dad. I'll never put you in a home."

CHAPTER 2

Day of Reckoning

Returning home late that afternoon, I relayed my father-daughter conversation to my children's father, Dave. Noticing an all-too-familiar bleeding-heart look in my eyes, the same look I gave him when I brought home a stray animal that needed loving or gave extra money to the homeless on a street corner, his obsidian eyes narrowed into paper-thin slits. Without hesitation, he announced firmly, "We're not taking care of your parents!"

"What if they need us?" I asked, fearing the confrontation.

"Nope, we're not doing it."

"But . . ."

"No, Jackie."

"I'd help you take care of your parents," I said, hoping to persuade him to come around to the idea.

"Do we have any beer? All I see is milk in here," he shouted, sticking his head in the refrigerator.

"Dave, did you hear me? I said I'd help take care of your parents."

"Where's the remote, I can't find it. You know the game is on tonight."

Determined to gain his attention, I declared, "I'm having a serious conversation here."

With an exhausted look, he attempted to be the voice of reason, "Jackie, we have our hands full with four kids; we're not taking care of anyone else."

"Wouldn't you want the kids to take care of you when you get old?"

"I'm not going to get old."

"What are you talking about? How can you say such a stupid thing?"

"Nope, I plan to die before I become like your parents. Is there any beer in the garage refrigerator?"

Tearfully, I turned away.

I always knew marriage would be a complicated union. We had met as dreamy-eyed young adults, barely in our twenties and ready to embark on a lifetime adventure together, a shimmering vow with dreams of prosperity, excitement, and healthy babies—in our case, lots of babies. But I forgot that nowhere in that oath did it say, "to love, honor, and cherish your in-laws in their sickness and health until they depart." Our lives together were meant to be just that: us together, with no external interference.

I tried again, delving into the reasons as to why this was so important to me.

"What if in the middle of the night, one of them got scared and there was no one to soothe them? You know Mom and Dad don't sleep together anymore since they both became crippled. Old people get nightmares too."

"Now you're being ridiculous."

"Well . . ."

"Jackie, I know you've got a good heart—that's why I love you. You always want to save the world, but we have to think about our lives. Now, where did you say you put the remote control?"

Turning his attention to a long evening of Monday night football, joystick firmly in hand, he ended the discussion with, "When the kids are out of the house, I want it to be just us. Besides, your parents were fine sticking your grandmother in a home."

While I hated to admit it, he had a point.

Nonetheless, I carried on. "Dave, you haven't seen that place. It's disgusting. All the people are slumped in their wheelchairs drooling, and there are bugs everywhere. I bet it's even infested with rats."

Without even a glance in my direction, he stonewalled me. Silence suffocated the room as he grabbed the remote and pointed it at the TV.

"Okay," I mumbled, realizing this was not a good time to push the idea any further. Throwing in the towel, I did my best Scarlet O'Hara impression. Despite the rage swelling in my heart, it was best to worry about it later.

Escaping to the grocery store, I fumed in private, feeling as if the subject had been stomped out like a discarded cigarette in the gutter, with no hope of re-igniting.

After collecting my berries, yogurt, and toilet paper, I found the longest line to stand in, just to kill more time before going home.

How could he not see how important this was to me? I get that they'd be an inconvenience, but isn't that what life's all about? Caring for those who need our help?

Gathering up my purchases, I drove home breathing deeply just like in Lamaze classes. They relieved pain during childbirth, why not the angst over aging parents? But as I pulled into the driveway, reality hit as I noticed our four-year-old on the roof, inches away from possibly careening to her death.

"Lauren, what are you doing up there?" I screamed at my baby girl, tiptoeing across the peak of the roof in bare feet. Like her three siblings, Lauren was a free spirit, but this child loved to trip the light fandango with absolutely no fear. Children, more than old parents, needed to be constantly watched.

"I'm looking for the ball, Mommy." She smiled, as if her death-defying location equaled the simple task of scrounging behind the elderberry bushes that grew at the front of our home. "I climbed the tree in the back to get here."

"Don't move! I'm coming to get you."

Dave was right. As a parent, I was on call every waking minute of every day (and well into the night) to not just the needs and desires of my four children, but keeping them out of mortal danger too. I had more on my plate than was manageable. How could I ever take care of my parents as well?

In those early child rearing days, I found myself constantly chasing my tail trying to keep everything moving in order. Each morning as I looked at the colorful dots on the calendar (each one representing a different child) letting me know their comings and goings of the day, I struggled to manage not only schedules, but cranky moods.

But at the end of the day—well, most days—I loved being a mother. I knew they were the greatest joys of my life.

Despite my four children coming from the same gene pool, each not only looked but acted dramatically different. Michelle, the oldest, was always the leader, strong and determined, setting the example for her siblings. She was my confidant from the moment she was born with a kind and empathetic nature. Polite, popular, and an overachiever in school, she danced semi-professionally for years, and cultivated an acting career in San Francisco during her high school years which she continued after college. There was nothing she touched that didn't turn out flawless and her siblings not only adored her but looked up to her.

Jenni was two years younger and while Michelle was tall, blonde and blue-eyed, Jenni was short, dark haired, hazel-eyed, and gentle in spirit. From the moment she was born, each day held magic and excitement for Jenni and could be witnessed by her squeals of laughter that bounced off the walls in our home with deafening volume. She loved fairytales, birthday parties (especially her own), Santa Claus, and the Easter Bunny. And, like her mother, she was a people pleaser and would do anything or give up even her prized possessions just to make someone else happy. If ever there was a model for the innocent child, that would be my dark-haired beauty.

Then there was the spirited one. Lauren's birth came as a surprise, just twenty months after Jenni. Regardless of the fact her father and I were using protection, this little bundle of energy was determined to be born and made herself known everywhere she went with her magnetic personality, amazing athletic ability, and fierce sense of humor. She began walking by eight months, and I spent her entire childhood racing to catch up to her. Without a fearful bone in her body, there was no tree too high to climb, no raging river too deep to swim across, and no garage door she couldn't hang onto as it went up and down. I often thought she would kill me one day from laughter or exhaustion.

Finally, there was the youngest, or as I lovingly referred to him, my "angel baby." Timmy—the beautiful child with his golden curls and deep blue eyes—was the easiest of all my children as a little person, sleeping through the night at six days old, and sweet in nature. Named after my second brother, as a toddler, he tended to the family dog and his mother with hugs and kisses to let us know we were loved. Later, he grew into a typical boy—mischievous, overly active, and constantly finding himself in trouble at school for being the class clown. During his grammar school years, I had many a meeting with his teachers over his desire to make others laugh at the expense of his learning in the classroom. But each time his contrite eyes looked into mine, my heart melted.

When my children were younger, I made life completely about them, forgetting that my aging parents even existed. I bent over backwards to make everything perfect, was on top of every need and whim while sacrificing any needs I might have, and fell into bed at night completely exhausted. To stay one step ahead of any verbal tongue lashing from any one of them because things weren't quite right, for I hated confrontation, I got through the day by running—figuratively, but running just the same.

"I feel like all I do is race through my life," I moaned to my friend, Linda, as I sat at her kitchen table a week later. As the mother of three daughters close in age to mine, I was sure she'd understand. "I run a taxi service. I run the family laundromat, bath water, vacuum cleaner, dishwasher, and dust buster."

"Oh, I know," she agreed. "I'm constantly on the go too. It all gets to be too much."

"It's like I'm a damn short order cook making heavily loaded carbohydrate meals for the athletes and hard-boiled eggs for the dieter. Each one is so picky about what they eat. And I'm always forgetting things at the store they claim they need. They're starting to catch on I might be lying when I say I forget."

"Really? How?"

"They wanted apples the other day. Typical, I forgot them and told them the store ran out."

"Ha! Nice try! What store runs out of apples?"

"That's what they said."

Pouring me another cup of coffee, Linda sat down next to me. "I don't know how you keep anything straight. Look at all you do: Women's Club president, cheerleading coach, art docent, softball coach, and dance instructor. If I ran that many miles in a day, I'd have serious blisters on my fatigue factor too."

In those crazy early years, long before I added real estate agent to the list of duties, every second of every hour was accounted for. I felt like I needed an oxygen tank just to catch a breath.

Just when I thought I was stretched to the max, 2000 became the year when life began to pour lighter fuel onto the already out of control bonfire. On top of my mother's cancer, back issues, and arthritis that made it hard for her to get around, the muscles that once held her intestines in place gave way. She was now dealing with a prolapsed rectum, which caused excruciating pain, bleeding, and many a mishap when it came to getting to the bathroom on time. Constant cries of "Jackie, I need you" over the phone left me feeling like a Duncan yo-yo that never stopped spinning as I drove a half hour each way, often several times a day, to bathe my parents, feed them, and run the errands they could no longer do themselves.

"Mom, where are your brothers?" Jenni asked one evening as I rushed in the door. "This just isn't fair."

"I'm sorry I'm late, honey. I had to be sure your grandparents had all they needed." Trying to diffuse her frustration, I explained, "Your uncles are too far away. Only I can do all this."

"Well, it's not fair. You do everything."

"I know it seems like that, but Grandma needs a lot of extra care now," I explained. "Her back surgery didn't work the way they hoped, and she's in constant pain. There's no way your grandfather can help. After his stroke, he can't do anything for himself."

Looking up from her homework, she suggested, "Why don't they hire someone so you can take a break?"

What a logical and simple solution, I thought. *Wouldn't it be nice if that were an option?*

But adults from the Great Depression didn't pay for anything they could take care of themselves. Or their children could take care of.

"I know this is hard on all of us, but please be patient. It won't last forever."

Then she had another perfect solution. "Have Dad help you."

Walking over to give her a kiss on the top of her innocent head, I said the only thing I could think of, "Your father's busy with work. Besides, they're not his parents."

By 2001, my life was frayed so thin that the tapestry of who I once was became a scrap of fabric with no design, no texture, and no worth. Instead, I was a shredded piece of material that was better used as a dust rag than a piece of art hung on the wall. I was a mess and exhausted, and life was about to get even messier.

CHAPTER 3

Enough is Enough

On July 20, 2003, a massive chunk of my father's enormous loving heart was ripped out of his chest by the greedy Angel of Death. Long before we were prepared, his life partner of fifty-five years was whisked away on spiked wings, leaving him isolated in an empty house. To deal with his loneliness, he wove an impenetrable cocoon around his aching memories. Twisting and turning in his mind, this already quiet man encased himself in prayer and shut himself off even further from the world.

The last two years had seen my life implode as well. In addition to the death of my sweet mother, my children left for college and their adult lives, and my marriage of twenty-two years fell apart. I was fifty-one years old living in a five-bedroom home and supporting myself with several jobs with flexible hours: a new career in real estate as well as a dance and fitness instructor, and an author with a column in the local newspaper. Not stuck in a desk nine to five, I was free to make choices about how I spent my time. Except for the companionship of our hyperactive pound puppy Maddie who we rescued in 2001, I was now all alone, and my father needed me. It was time to make good on my thirteen-year-old promise.

"Dad, I think it's time you considered moving in with me,"

I said gently to him shortly after my mother's funeral. "I don't like the idea of you being all alone in this big house."

Determined to hang onto his independence, he did what he typically did when avoiding a subject he didn't want to discuss. He harrumphed and placed the San Francisco Chronicle's sporting green in front of his face.

"Dad, we need to talk about this."

"There's nothing to say," he grumbled. "I'm not paying someone just to sit around all day."

Casting around for a gentle way to show Dad that he needed help, I noticed his disheveled appearance. My father had always been fastidious about his appearance. Each morning began with a shower and a shave, followed by getting dressed in a starched shirt and pressed pants. His outfit alone told me he could not live alone anymore.

"Dad, who dressed you this morning?" Teasing, I rebuttoned his shirt.

"What's that supposed to mean," he groused, irritated. "Me, of course."

"Do you know you have on different colored socks, and I hate to tell you this, but you need to pull up your zipper."

Struggling to guide the slider over two rows of jagged metal teeth, his frustration escalated. Pulling harder and harder but going nowhere, he gave up.

"What does it matter? No one comes to visit me."

"I'm here," I reminded him, trying to reduce his dejected feelings.

Silence.

Besides the fact that getting dressed had regressed him to a two-year-old, where clothing was picked without thought, there was the issue of personal cleanliness. A shower on his own was no longer a possibility as he needed help getting in and out. Preparing food had become dangerous—he tended to forget the stove was on. On top of that, his left arm was useless and his mobility had slowed to a turtle's labored crawl. Whatever he prepared for himself would be cold and unpalatable by the time he made it to the table to sit and eat.

"Dad," I began, calming my nerves with a large swallow of air but wishing it was a glass of Chardonnay. "I want you to have the life you desire, but I can't be here every day to help you."

He was as unresponsive as the granite statue of St. Francis in our garden, so I carefully pulled back the Chronicle. His bushy eyebrows lay pinched on the bridge of his nose, and eighty-six years of expression lines were tightly tugged into a pursed frown.

"I know you don't want to live with me yet, and I respect that, but you have to give me a little help here."

Pulling the paper out of my fingers, the daily news rose like the Great Wall of China, repelling all invaders and daughters with bad ideas.

"No, Jackie. I don't want it."

Over the course of my life as daddy's little girl, I learned when to force an issue or when to fold. Seeing he had his cards tight to his chest, this was going to be a long game of poker before I could make him throw in his hand.

Leaving his side, I went about my duties as the new woman of the house. There was laundry to wash, a layer of dust to erase off the furniture, vacuuming to do, linens to change, bills to pay, and food to prepare for later.

Sensing his eyes peeking above the green paper, I played my best Greta Garbo with heavy sighs of exasperation as I pushed the old Hoover past his chair, sucking up weeks of dirt out of the green shag carpet. Watching his only daughter work too hard always softened his heart. He could be a pain at times, but not at the expense of his sweet little rosebud—his rose among my three thorny brothers.

"Okay, okay. You can hire someone, but only to get me in and out of bed. No sleepovers."

"Thanks, Dad!" Kissing him on the cheek, I proclaimed, "I'll get on it right away."

In California's Silicon Valley, the Tongan community had developed support groups for the care of the aging. Originally from the South Pacific, these men and women carried with them a deep respect and love for family and religion. While we Americans held youth, independence, and skinny girls in bikinis in high regard, Tongans respected and revered their elders. Who better than a robust Islander to help me with my father?

"Dad, I think I may have found the right fit for you," I began one morning as I stripped his mattress of soiled linens. "I interviewed her yesterday. She helped my friend Debi with her mother-in-law when she was sick and is now available. Her name is Rena."

"Did they fire her?"

"No, Dad, they didn't fire her. Why do you ask?"

"Well, if she's so great, then why did they let her go? You just don't let good help go."

"Debi's mother-in-law is now in heaven."

Hearing that another soul was called home, he slumped in his chair.

"Oh. That's too bad." Then, as he looked outside the window, I heard in a low tone, "Okay, we can try her out."

Rena Fuenta, a massive, hairy, wild boar of a woman with solid gold teeth arrived a day later. Built like a Hummer in a colorful sarong, I was sure she could hold back an entire line of 49er defensive linemen if necessary while performing her duties as a vocational licensed nurse.

"I never knew a woman could be that strong or scary looking," I said to Debi, calling her to thank her for the referral. "Her teeth have enough gold to make a wearable piece of jewelry."

"Is she good to your dad?" Debi questioned.

"Yes, very sweet."

"Good. Then you can get past her looks."

At five foot ten, Rena took complete control of all his needs—cleaning his bottom when accidents occurred, feedings, meds, and adjusting his ragdoll body into whatever position needed. Her massive girth and vigor, coupled with scientific knowledge about momentum and inertia, looked at ease catapulting his 180-pound, six-foot frame from one chair to the another and back into bed at the end of the day.

"What do you think, Dad?" I asked one evening on a visit home.

"She's all right."

Knowing full well she was doing a great job, I responded, "Just all right?"

"She'll do, for now."

In the beginning, all went swimmingly. Like my childhood goldfish Peaches swirling lazily in circles in her clear glass bowl without a care in the world, I could relax and just come when I wanted to spend time with my father.

Rena doted on Dad's every whim, from ice cream sundaes for breakfast to the volume set on full blast on the TV. She fluffed his pillows, bathed his body, sang him religious melodies, and wiped the drool from his sagging lips. She also made promises.

"Jack, I'll always be here with you. You'll never need to find anyone else to care for you."

"Promise?" he asked like a child wanting another bedtime story if he brushed his teeth.

"I promise!"

But some promises can't help but be broken when the sirens of money croon their hypnotic tune. Living on a fixed income, Dad only had so much discretionary cash for his care. At eighty-eight, his savings were beginning to wane and he planned to live to one hundred. Therefore, a strict budget was mandatory if he was not to become a burden on his children. Unfortunately, the call of the almighty dollar is an evil we can all get sucked into. After one year with my dad, Rena left for a more lucrative position, dissolving her vow and leaving a sad heart as she closed the door behind her.

"She knew what I could pay when she took the job. She promised she'd never leave."

"I know, Dad. I'm sorry you're upset, but we'll find you someone else."

"I should have never let you talk me into all this. It only ends in disappointment."

Thinking this might be my big chance, I asked again, "Would you like to live with me now?"

With his remote firmly in his grip, he changed channels on the TV at lightning quick speed. To avoid any further discussion, he ratcheted up the volume.

"Dad, did you hear me?" I yelled close to his ear.

Long seconds dragged as the wheels turned behind his blue eyes. Then, as if the angel of mercy couldn't take it any longer, he hit the mute button.

"I have a better idea. You sell your house and come live with me."

"Ah, no." I replied. "My life is in Los Altos."

As a writer, I've been programmed to watch for that flicker of consciousness when you truly see a person and their idiosyncrasies. That flash of "aha!" clarity. This was one of those moments.

Just like me, my father loved his home. It was where he felt safe and housed all his happy memories of growing babies, a beautiful wife to meet him at the end of his busy day, and a sanctuary from a world that could be unkind. Of course, he didn't want to leave it.

"Okay, but we need to find someone else to help."

A week later, in walked the second string.

Enemi Helu, a short but powerfully built mother of four, quickly picked up where Rena left off.

"Enemi, how are you able to move him the way you do?" I asked as I watched her lift him like an oversized bag of sugar. "You're so much shorter than I am."

"Yeah, but I'm strong," she said lifting her thick ham hock arm and patting the well-developed bulge of her bicep.

Not only could Enemi maneuver my father's deadweight body throughout the house and get him to his doctor visits, but she also performed all the daily tasks for a salary that didn't drain his bank account.

She also made a promise to stay with him to the end. We hoped that this time, it was a vow that would be kept.

After six years of fairly smooth sailing with Enemi at the helm of my father's care, the low rumble that comes before the enormous shock waves began, slowly disintegrating my childhood home into a pile of rubble. Unfortunately, what began as a foundation built on bedrock gradually liquefied like loose sand and dirt that mixes with ground water during an earthquake. While Dad's physical needs were met, housekeeping was a different story.

"Holy shit!" I blurted in horror as I walked into my dad's house one Wednesday morning. Panicking that his bills needed to be paid promptly (like the moment they arrived at the house), he wanted me there every day. "What happened? It looks like a tornado hit."

Roaming from room to room, I saw piles of unfolded laundry were stacked over chairs, on beds, and in corners. It looked as if Enemi waited for a month to pass before washing his clothes. But I knew that wasn't true—Dad didn't even have this many clothes.

"When did Dad start wearing flowered panties?" I mumbled, picking up a pair of elephant-sized unmentionables. Studying the mountain of cotton, it was obvious that the oversized Kmart undies, florescent tank tops, and paisley printed skirts belonged to anyone but Dad. Somehow, my father's house had turned into a laundromat.

Things had gone adequately for so long, but somehow a new arrangement had been made, one my father and I were never told about.

What I began to understand was that Enemi was not the greatest of poor housekeepers. While she tried, her version of cleanliness and mine were on opposite ends of the broom handle. She was now living full time with Dad and had begun to feel comfortable enough to see our home as her home, inviting her extended family over. However, it seems that this included the entire freaking village! Before I knew it, strangers were taking over every room—her "uncles and aunts" having the run of the house when my father was in bed, and sometimes when he was in his chair right in the living room. Quickly, I called for reinforcements.

"David, I think she's doing the wash for the entire church," I said, calling my older brother for advice. "What do I do?"

David was the firstborn in the Madden family, the brother we all looked up to because of his wisdom and higher education. Obtaining a PhD in English literature, he was as well-read as our parents, equally bright, and always seemed to have the answers for any problem.

"Ask Dad."

"Ask Dad? How would he know? I think he can barely see. I bet he doesn't even know they're here half the time."

"Well, it sounds suspicious. You better keep a close eye."

I tried, but each time I arrived it seemed to get worse. Rotund brown bodies wrapped in colorful prints lurked in every room, grinning like Cheshire cats (in need of a good orthodontist) who'd just eaten a juicy mouse. The washing machine never stopped gyrating.

"Dad! Who are all these people?" I whispered loudly into his good ear. It was getting out of control.

Shrugging his shoulders, he looked out the window to the creek across the street, watching a quail wiggling her little body.

"Your mother used to love those birds."

"Dad, I'm talking humans! People are all over the place with gold teeth and sumo-type bodies."

Staring back at the daughter who was obviously bothering him, he said, "She says they're her cousins."

"By the looks of things, her family was rather fertile."

Each time I came to visit my dad, another offense was added to my growing list. Being a woman who typically does a slow burn to get her pot boiling, I was now at 212 degrees Fahrenheit.

Finally, during one visit in May 2011, I reached a rolling boil. Standing in the kitchen, I choked back a gag at the odor of rotting shredded pork and mushy cabbage, which reminded me of the days I shared the hall bathroom with my three brothers. The musty smells of athletic bodies lingering on the damp towels and in toilets that were never flushed were fragrances I didn't want to revisit in my adult years, yet here we were again—only now it was in the hub of food preparation.

Floating in the middle of my mom's favorite cut glass crystal bowl on the kitchen table was a shriveled black turd-like log.

I leaned over the disgusting substance and took a whiff.

"Crap! What is that?"

If there was one thing I knew in life, it was feces. Between my four children's smelly bottoms, a dog that had no idea what "outside" meant, and a mother with no bowel control near the end, I was the queen of cleaning up shit.

Immobilized, I stared, wondering what the thing was and afraid to find out.

On the kitchen counter, bananas and mangos rotted in the pink vase my mother once filled with sweet smelling roses from her garden. Stacked in the sink was her good china, dried food petrified to the hand-painted poppies. And, on the filthy floor, a dead cockroach who couldn't escape fast enough lay on its back, tiny legs stiff and frozen mid-kick, as if reaching for the ceiling to escape the madness.

Enemi used to be diligent with keeping things up. Maybe she was too distracted entertaining all her guests, but this had to change.

To say I was pissed was only a partial expression of the resentment building inside of me. The carpets hadn't been vacuumed in weeks, dust was covering every piece of furniture in volcanic thickness, and black mold was creeping up the walls of the bathtub.

I'd been there the day before but hadn't noticed the filth. My focus had been centered on my father and the puddle of urine he was laying in on his bed. I soon realized that adult diapers would be the solution for future leakage problems.

Fire and rage surged in my veins. I thought my head was about to explode. My dad was being taken advantage of.

All that would have been manageable except for the words that slipped through his lips as I sat down next to him. I gave him a soft kiss on the cheek to let him know I was there.

"I'm a little depressed."

I'm not surprised, I thought, but I waited for him to tell me why.

"I never get ice cream anymore."

I sat stunned as if someone had just thrown water in my face to get my attention. The one thing my father loved was his ice cream after dinner. It was a staple in our home, just like flour, milk, and sugar.

"What do you mean, you don't get ice cream?"

Fingering the tissue on his chest to catch the drool that dripped from his gaping mouth as he slept his day away, he sighed. "She's too busy to buy it."

"Excuse me?" I exclaimed, flabbergasted. "With all these people in our house, there's no excuse for someone not to go and buy you ice cream."

"I ask for it every day, but she says she doesn't have time. I think she just forgets."

I was livid.

"That's not okay! I'm going to have a word with her," I bellowed.

"No, no. Just leave it alone," Dad answered, his voice hushed so as not to be heard. Hating confrontation, he'd rather suffer in silence than do anything about it. Besides, he felt safe in her arms whenever she lifted him in and out of bed and I knew he didn't want to lose that security. But enough was enough. Something had to change.

"That's it, Dad. We're not doing this anymore."

I gently turned his sad face in my direction so he could absorb every word I was about to say to him.

"We've done all this long enough. I'm giving you one month to wrap your mind around the fact that you're coming to live with me."

I understood my dad's need to be independent was something I should respect, but it was time for a change.

"If you come to my house, I promise you'll have everything you need and want. You will have ice cream every day."

In this tired moment, his rheumy eyes looked into mine, and he softly uttered, "Okay, but what about Enemi?"

When Enemi moved in with Dad two years before it had

been a win-win situation. Up to that point, she'd arrive at 9:00 a.m., do her routine and leave at 6:00 p.m. once he was settled in bed. Knowing he was lying alone for all those hours gave me many a sleepless night, but he refused to pay for more care.

But when a stint in the hospital left him under the watchful eye of the caseworkers, 24-hour care was mandated. Enemi's husband had recently left her and her daughter for another woman, taking the younger son with him, and she needed a place to live. Dad needed more help, but didn't want to pay for it. Enemi and her child moved in and she was only paid for the daytime hours.

"Maybe we can find a way to keep her, but only to work for you. She can see her cousins after hours."

June 1, 2011, became the due date for what I anticipated would be a new life of peace, love, protection, and after dinner sweets. A month would give us both time to prepare—for him to let go and ready himself for the final stage of his life, and for me to figure out how to fulfill a promise that would soon feel like my great undoing.

CHAPTER 4

Preparing the House

For over the past seven years, my father's body had mostly been sequestered to a fabric cell in the shape of a frayed recliner with decaying walls of green plaid closing in around him. Unable to move on his own, he spent his days staring out a wall of glass, watching birds flapping their wings on the tips of dancing trees, all keeping perfect step with the melody of the wind. I could see by the look in his eyes how he longed for the day when he'd be free to fly too.

While my heart ached for his situation, I knew living with me would be much better than the isolation he'd been experiencing. Other than the weekly visit from a member of the church to bring him communion, there was no mental stimulation from visitors to ask about his day, what was on his mind, or what memories he had hidden deep within. Despite the fact a Tongan army had descended upon his quiet sanctuary, no one thought to interact with him. They were too busy cackling in the kitchen to care that an old man sat by himself every day, staring out the window.

As I thought about my father's life, it became apparent that moving him would entail bringing very little.

"Dad," I said, gently tapping his arm to get his attention, "I want you to think about what you want to bring with you."

Turning his gaze from the world outside, he studied my face as if I were speaking in a foreign tongue.

"I changed my mind," he gruffly said. "I want to stay here."

At times, Dad could act like a petulant child, holding his ground until he got his way. Unfortunately for him, this was one argument I planned to win.

"Dad, we've already discussed this. You can't live here anymore, so you better start thinking about what's important to bring with you."

Giving me an annoyed look, his eyebrows furloughed into narrow grooves that hung so low they seemed to rest on the tip of his nose. "Women . . ." he grumbled.

From my perspective, what to bring would be easy. His life had become minimalistic. There'd be no need for fancy suits, jackets, and ties. Each day followed the same pattern: sponge bath in bed, dressed in comfy sweatpants and a golf shirt, brown socks with Velcro shoes, breakfast at the kitchen table, and then plopped into his chair for endless hours where he thought about God knows what. Later in the day, the order was meticulously reversed.

To maintain this lifestyle, all he'd need was his hospital-issued bed, walker and cane, TV with headphones, and a picture or two. Fifty-two years of his life at 112 Windsor Drive, San Carlos, could easily fit into two small boxes.

"Dad, would you like me to walk you through the house to look at things you want to take?"

He made no eye contact as he brushed me off. "No, you know what I'll need."

With his eyes glued again to the world beyond the window, I was sure there were things he'd want with him. But what worried me more was that he'd be leaving behind items he didn't get to give a proper farewell to.

There would be the "goodbye" to the scarlet rose bush outside his bedroom window that he planted when we first moved in 1959, still effortlessly blooming in vibrant shades of red in the spring and summer. I would expect a teary-eyed "cheerio" to the sandbox that once called to his four children and years later, his eight grandchildren. Now, it just crooned to the neighborhood cats as a spot to relieve their bladders during an evening prowl.

And I was sure there'd be an emotional "toodle-loo" to the mountain of books waiting to be devoured, books he'd received as gifts but sat unopened. I had yet to understand that the macular degeneration had already poured a film over his eyes, leaving his vision blurred and the written word undetectable.

There'd be an "adios" to the kitchen table where the family once congregated in high spirits for a meal and discussion. Long ago there were talks of politics, school grades, matters of faith, and the current events of his young and restless children as they prepared for their futures. Now, all that remained was a seat for one.

But the saddest "farewell" would be to the bedrooms where his children once slept. Despite the fact we no longer lived there, he still acted as the castle's sentinel: the graying knight safeguarding his holy grail, rolling slowly by each evening on his way to the lonely tower he once shared with my mother. Passing each doorway, he'd say a silent prayer for our continued safety in a world he perceived no longer needed him.

Yes, in my mind, a month was plenty of time to make peace with it all. What I didn't realize was that it was I who would require a course in time management to prepare. My home had been built for children getting ready to fly the coop, not molting chickens stuck in their cages.

"There are so many things I need to do to get ready for your grandfather," I told my youngest, Timmy, on a rare visit home from his life in San Francisco as he was watching the 49ers play the Rams. With all my children out of the house, and me wanting their opinion whenever I could grab it, I continued, "I want to make sure he'll have everything he needs."

"Mom, I don't know why you're so worried. His life is pretty simple."

"I know, but what if I forget something? I want him to feel as if this is his home."

"You need to relax. He should be happy with whatever you do for him. At least you're not sticking him in a home."

True, but I often wondered why some of life's major decisions were easy for others to take in stride and not me. Maybe it was because I was the one most affected. Friends and family got to go on their merry way while I was left with an aging soul.

"I know this may sound simple to you, but I want him to be comfortable. He's used to looking out a window to watch the birds," I said, trying to express my need to have everything right. "I have no idea where to put that ugly chair he loves. If I put it in the living room, it'll be the first thing people see when they come in."

Looking up from the game, my child shot me his exasperated look of frustration that I knew all too well when I overcomplicated a simple matter.

"Just put it by the sliding glass door here in the family room. He'll be close to the TV if he ever wants to watch it and he can look at those stupid birds all he wants."

In its youth, the recliner, made of fine Ethan Allen construction, was inviting and pristine. But due to the daily battle of loading and unloading my dad's broken body, the seams were splitting apart, exposing the stained, spongy foam within. Where his feet rested, the fabric had been ripped away as his leg brace sawed against the grain of fabric.

"Mom, it's just a chair," my baby boy, now twenty-three-years old, continued as he noticed I wasn't paying attention to him. "What does it matter where you put it?"

"It's so gross! I bet if I left it out on the street with a sign that said 'free,' not even a homeless person would want it."

"Get over yourself and stop worrying about it."

He did have a point. Next to the sliding door was a better solution than the living room.

But despite the fact the chair had now found a home, there was still much planning left to do. Unfortunately, no matter how many times I made a list and checked it a million times, I felt like something was missing. Like I was planning a big birthday celebration but had forgotten to send out the invitations.

By government standards, my dad was deemed handicapped, and as such, the rules and regulations that guide the safety of others from disabled individuals became his undoing. Because he'd become challenged in his gait, the DMV took his license away in 2006 when he was eighty-eight. I suppose it was a good thing since he was bumping into other cars, but it broke his heart. Besides the question of how he would get to Mass every day, the last shred of independence he owned had been ripped away.

Along with ways to protect those around him, laws are in place that require buildings used by disabled individuals to have stress-free entry. The Bill of Rights declares we all are guaranteed the right to "Life, Liberty, and the Pursuit of Easy Accessibility." In other words, I'd be forced to build a wheelchair ramp for him, one of those ugly platforms placed over perfectly designed steps that destroy the curb appeal of any home.

Later that day, twenty-nine-year-old Michelle, who was visiting from Los Angeles, came home from shopping at the Stanford mall and found me standing in the gutter, staring at the front of the house, deep in thought.

"Mom, is something wrong?" she asked, clutching her purchases and passing me on her way to the front door.

"I just can't bring myself to stick one of those things on the front porch," I moaned. "They're so tacky."

"What thing?"

"One of those ugly metal ramps for Grandpa's wheelchair. My house will look like a nursing home."

"So . . ."

"So, you don't understand. I've worked hard to keep my home looking pretty."

"All right, but how do you think you're going to get him in and out of the house?"

Studying the situation, I found myself deep in thought. There has to be another way. It's not like he has a social life or anything.

"Mom, are you coming inside?"

Helping her with her bags, we walked in together as my quest continued. Placing her items on the kitchen counter, I began wishing I could build an undetectable escape route, an invisible door I could reveal with a snap to my fingers. Then, snapping twice, it would evaporate once the job was complete, leaving my house just the way I wanted it—wheelchair-ramp free.

"I don't understand why having a ramp is such a big deal," Michelle said as she unloaded her new clothes.

"I know it's silly," I agreed. "I just want what I want."

Just then, my eyes traveled to the sliding glass door where I had decided Dad's chair would be parked and I got a marvelous idea.

"I can build one over there," I shouted, pointing to an area just outside the door.

"Yeah, then what?" Her eyebrows raised into perfectly shaped arches. "So, you can get him in the backyard, but what if you want to take him for a walk or need to rush him to the hospital? You're going to have to wheel him around the side of the house where the garbage cans are, just to get him into the front yard."

"Well . . ."

"Mom, what if it's raining?"

As a mother, I've been well trained to answer any question my brood might pose, even the tough ones.

"If it's raining, I'll just wait for it to stop before we go."

"Mom!"

"Okay, okay. I'll buy a really big umbrella. I'm not putting a ramp in front of the house."

"You're crazy."

And, with a shake of her blonde head and a kiss to my cheek, out the kitchen she went.

Now that the solution was solved for the exterior, the interior became my next country to conquer. There'd be drawers and cabinets to clear out for his special food: canned peaches and pears, endless bags of Quaker Instant Oatmeal, and red licorice. Lots of red licorice.

The kitchen shouldn't be a problem, but where do I stick all the junk he has in his bathroom? He has more creams and lotions than I do.

Once upon a messy childhood, the hall bathroom was in a constant shape of chaos. There my four children did their business to get ready for the day—shampooed their bodies and hair, coiffed the follicles with hairspray and gel, picked at their skin an inch away from the mirror, and clogged the sink with enough hair to stuff a couch. The moment they left, it took a fire hose to wash it down.

The grungy, soap scum-stained sink and shower now sparkled. Where forest green towels once hung (chosen to hide all the stains), immaculate white ones lined with green satin were perfectly folded on towel bars to be used only as decorations. The toilet bowl stayed Lysol fresh, and lavender-grapefruit candles filled the air with an intoxicating aroma. Now, with dad's sanitary wipes and adult diapers, I'd be thrown in a time machine back twenty years. Back to the days of Pampers and poop.

I didn't think this all through very well, I thought, going from room to room, digesting how things were about to become different. I'd just gotten this place looking the way I wanted. So much was about to change.

Then, realizing there was a massive hurdle I hadn't considered, I poured myself a drink of wine. Despite the fact I had a five-bedroom house, someone was about to be bumped to make room for Daddy. This would prove to be one of the most difficult decisions.

CHAPTER 5

Child Displacement

The bedroom is the room in a house where we go to relax in, to store our personal belongings, and to fantasize about our futures. If a child is truly lucky, as in my case, it's a private space that belongs to them and them alone. Boys need not enter, and parents only after knocking. It's a hallowed domain where memories are created and revisited. No one ever told me how painful it would be to lose my bedroom.

At the age of seven, when we moved to our second home on Windsor Drive, I was given the privilege of no longer sharing a sleeping space with my brothers. Gone were the trucks and soldiers, dirty socks that smelled of wet grass and mud, and the messy beds where the art of hospital corners became lost. For as long as I could remember, every night there had been a lump of testosterone snoring two feet away from me. I now could fill the room with dolls, keep the vases full of fresh flowers from the garden, and arrange my stuffed animals in an orderly fashion across my pillow. But, most importantly, I was to be left alone.

I can't believe I have my own room, my young mind cheered as I sat on the edge of my bed and looked around. *I'm going to make sure it's always pretty.*

For the next two years, this small chamber inside the Madden castle was a hodgepodge of mismatched furniture: a green dresser that once held baby clothes, a faded yellow desk that was resurrected from my maternal grandmother's basement, and a heavy black headboard with tall, carved posts that had been handed down from one generation to another.

While the rest of the house received brand new salt-and-pepper tweed carpet, the funds ran out by the time they got to my room. There lay a slab of forest green carpet pulled up from our previous home on Arundel Road, complete with the stains young children make.

There were no frills, no lacy curtains or feminine bedspread with throw pillows in shades of the pink and blue of my dreams. And, because I was so young, a mirror was not yet necessary. There was still plenty of time for such embellishment. But, despite the fact the décor looked like something out of the Goodwill bargain basement, I loved it.

"Isn't our new home beautiful?" I asked my baby dolls as they sat around their tiny wooden table in their chairs. "Remember to be polite and no messes. I want this to stay just as it is."

It was between those four walls where I found myself in control, for once in my life. Being outnumbered in the gender department got tiring. God gave the Madden males a larger set of lungs, and they were always heard first. Not wanting to fight to be noticed, I spent hours playing with my dolls, moving them around the menagerie; one day it was mothering Raggedy Ann and Andy and the other children in the nursery, the next, Barbie and Ken ruled the floor as they drove in circles in her peach-colored convertible coupe. Peace and order reigned, never again to be interrupted by clumsy sneakers making their

way through my playground as they carelessly stepped on a
few napping plastic dolls.

After two years of saving all their spare change, my
parents finally had enough money to buy me real furniture and
a new rug: a beautiful honey-colored maple bedroom set like
something out of a Drexel furniture catalog, and snow-white
carpet.

Under the window that looked out at the willow tree next
door sat my twin bed covered in a white bedspread and yellow
and green pillows for a splash of color. A nightstand held my
rosebud hurricane lamp, pink AM radio, and nighttime book
of the week. Against the large wall was a double dresser with
enough drawers to house not only winter and summer clothes
but all four seasons, as well as an enormous mirror for one day
applying makeup. In the corner sat a lovely grown-up desk
with five drawers for all my creative writing supplies and
journals.

Where once there was just a pane of glass, dainty white
curtains trimmed in eyelet lace were hung with a shade I could
pull shut so the neighbors wouldn't be able to see my budding
body change. And, on the walls, pink, green, and yellow Monet-
like flowers scattered over the wallpaper.

"Oh, Mom and Dad, I love it. Thank you!" I exclaimed when
it was done, my nine-year-old self absolutely thrilled with the
room makeover. I threw my arms around them both as they
stood with me to look at their handiwork. "I promise to keep it
looking like this forever."

A promise I would keep for the next seventeen years.

As the years sped by, my room became my demilitarized
zone where I could act like Switzerland when the heated

discussion on whose NFL team was the best or who would make it to the World Series became too much.

"Jackie," my father called, tapping first before entering. "Why don't you come out with the rest of the family?"

"No thanks, Dad. You guys are watching sports. I'll stay here."

"But you're always in your room. We'd love to have you with us."

"Can we watch The Patty Duke show?" I asked, already knowing the answer.

Smiling, he patted my head. "That might cause a war."

"I'm good, but thanks for asking me."

Private bedrooms have a way of making sense of the world outside when life gets confusing. They soothe emotions as yet another pimply faced boy breaks your heart or when facing a difficult test in math the following day. A bedroom is where you aspire for greatness in your future or cry your tears about present failures. But, in 1981, after I'd been out of the house for nearly nine years and married for two, all that changed.

"Jackie, Grandma needs to live with us," I remember my mother saying on the other end of the phone as if she was announcing there'd be chicken for dinner again. "She'll be staying in your room."

"Really?" I tried to process what was being said.

"The doctor said she couldn't live alone anymore and I can't bear to put her away. I'm giving her your room."

Stunned, I sat silent for a second, and then blurted, "Where am I supposed to sleep?"

"What do you mean, 'where will you sleep?' You don't live here anymore."

"Yeah, but it's still my room."

"Jackie, you can't be serious?" she said, a perturbed note in her voice. "You haven't lived here since high school, and you're married, for God's sake. Your place is with your husband."

While this was a true statement, even married women like to escape their reality from time to time and go back to the one place they never doubted they were loved.

"I know," I said, fearful tears might start to come. "But I come home a lot."

"I can't believe we're having this conversation. Your grandmother deserves a pretty room, and the boys' rooms are disgusting."

While the good girl inside understood that my parents were trying to do right by Grandma, it was still my room!

I wanted to scream, "Stop being so damn cheap and fix up one of the others! I still come home once in a while," but instead, I softened my tone and asked, now ashamed, "What if I want to come and visit? Where will I sleep?"

"You can always sleep in Michael's room."

Thinking about the 1970s time warp across the hall, with its burnt orange bedspread, avocado green shag carpet, and the stench of body odor and illegal smoke from funny cigarettes still imprinted deep into the bedspread, I saw my days of coming home to reconnect with myself would soon be over.

"Thanks. I'll keep that in mind."

Hanging up the phone, I searched my soul as to why this was so difficult for me to accept. After all, I was twenty-seven, pregnant with Michelle, married, and living in San Diego. Truth be told, I only came home by myself three or four times a year. Then it hit me. All my life, the only place I didn't have to fight to call my own was my bedroom. In college and post-graduate days I had roommates, and now I shared my living space with my husband. But I adored my grandmother and had to learn to accept things would be different.

And different they immediately became.

On my first visit home after the new arrangement, my mother asked as I walked through the door if I could help clean up. Grandma was sitting in the living room and Mom was doing her linens, but apparently there'd been some spillage.

Opening the door to my once beautiful, private space, I was hit with the smell of a diaper that had been left to stand in its juices and debris an hour too long.

Holy shit, I wanted to scream but tightened my lips. The space that had always been kept pristine looked like something out of an abandoned nursing home.

What happened?

It hadn't taken long for my desk to become cluttered with her medicines, a pill for every ache, every pain, and every rise and fall in blood pressure. Water rings dulled the sheen of the furniture I once lovingly polished. And instead of my white bedspread with a daisy crocheted afghan as the focal point, a port-a-potty sat center stage in the middle of the room with urine droplets and remnants of feces doing a Jackson Pollock splatter dance on the once-white carpet.

Tears began to sting my eyes, partly because this was not how I had left my room, but mostly because I now understood how the aging process degraded one's dignity into nothing.

"I can't believe how much has exploded from that tiny body of hers," I mumbled, lifting the bowl filled with bodily waste and carrying it to the bathroom. "I don't think multiple bottles of Clorox bleach will ever get the smell out of here."

After sterilizing and scrubbing the floor, I noticed stains on the mattress as well. No wonder my mother was doing so much laundry every day. My poor grandmother, once an elegant, sophisticated silent movie actress, had been reduced to an infant, needing those who loved her to clean up the mess.

Finishing my job, I went to the living room to see her staring out the window, humiliation and weathered hands covering her face. From the moment she was born until she turned ninety-two, she had been self-sufficient. Now, she was just another old soul waiting to die. So was my room.

"Hi Grammy. Can I read you something from the news-paper?" I asked, trying to deflect her embarrassment.

As I was preparing for Dad's arrival, these memories came roaring to the surface as if an oil well had been punctured deep within my past. Gushing forth uncontrollably, the pain resurfaced, and I was hit with the realization I was about to do this to one of my kids too.

I had to think about this logically. *It has to be the easiest room for Dad, and whoever that affects, they'll just have to under-stand.*

Closing my eyes, I visualized our two-story ranch with its five bedrooms and all the key players. Carefully lifting off the roof of the perfectly scripted dwelling where everyone had their bedroom, I mentally picked up the precious dolls and began rearranging their bodies onto different beds.

Studying Michelle's room on the second floor, it became immediately obvious that it couldn't be an option. I'd never be able to manage my dad's wheelchair up and down the staircase.

"Okay, that takes one out of the mix," I said softly, as I placed her back in her room in my mind's eye. Peering at the rooms below, another member would immediately be given dispensation as well due to his sex.

Timmy had spent twenty-three years surrounded by three sisters and a nagging mother. I couldn't expect him to give up his living quarters. Like me, it was his sanctuary to guard against raging female hormones. That wouldn't be just unfair, but cruel.

"That leaves Jenni or Lauren."

Sadly for Jenni, it quickly became apparent that her old room was the most logical solution with its easy access to the family room. I just had to find a way to become saleswoman of the year and make her believe it was her idea all along.

"You're giving him my room? Why not one of the others?" Jenni sounded somewhat annoyed when I called her to tell her.

Startled by the sound of magma beginning to boil on the other end of the phone, I did my best to divert the building eruption.

"Honey, it's just for a little while," I began, twisting my hair around my index finger. I knew she might be upset, but I was completely thrown off by the intensity of her reaction. "Your grandfather's ninety-five. It won't be forever."

"That's what your parents told you when your grandmother invaded your room, and she lived to 101!"

Yes, Jenni was right. Some senior citizens are born with a genetic makeup on steroids. Like the trick candles on a birthday cake, no matter how hard life blew on her, my grandmother's life would not be extinguished. She had seemed to be on a mission to outlive her entire legacy.

"And what about all my stuff?"

You mean all those boxes of letters, stuffed animals, photographs, and picture albums you've been saving since you were ten? I thought, but said, "I'll find them a safe place in the garage."

"Not just that, my clothes. Where will I put them?"

"Jenni, we'll find room for your things," I said, now a bit irritated. "There'll always be a bed for you here and a place to hang your clothes. Just think about it," I said as I shifted my body weight, unprepared for such an in-depth interrogation. "How often are we all together anyway? Thanksgiving. Christmas. Any other time, it won't be an issue."

But my reassurance fell on deaf ears.

"You know, Mom, he'll ruin my room. Remember how you said yours was never the same again?"

"Honey, mine was never the same because your grandparents refused to do anything to it after Grandma was gone," I responded, now borderline fuming. "When your grandfather no longer needs it, we'll re-do everything."

Like Pollyanna, I was not about to let this conversation spoil my decision. I'd play the Glad Game and look for all the positives.

"And you can help me by choosing colors and bed linens. It'll be a fun project," I chirped in my cheery, singsong way.

But rather than being the sweet, pliable child I knew so well, the people-pleasing clone of her mother, obstinacy rang in her responses. Volleying back and forth my reasons for and her questioning why her, a smoldering heat rose in my gut, an emotion I always tried to push down—anger.

Why should I even have to explain this? my thoughts screamed as I gritted my teeth in irritation. *This is my house. I pay the bills. No one helps me. I should be able to decide what to do with it.*

But I didn't say that. Instead, feeling defeated, I kept my mouth shut.

What infuriated me most was that this was not a life sentence. Just like my grandmother, one day, Dad would be gone too. The only difference was Jenni would get a whole new room out of it.

Soon the whimpering on the other end of the phone turned into convulsing sobs. My annoyance with the entire conversation now turned into disbelief.

"Jenni! What's wrong?"

"I don't mean to be selfish. I know this is something that has to be done, but . . ."

A stagnating pause asphyxiated the airwaves.

"Jenni? Are you there?" A sob. "Jenni, what's wrong?"

Clearing her throat and blowing her nose into what I hoped were tissues and not her sleeve, the real reason she was holding back spluttered out. "God, Mom! What if he dies in there? I'll never be able to sleep in my room again."

Adrenalin ignited like a flame on a gas stove. I was no longer angry. I was pissed.

I couldn't believe she just said that. Yes, it was shitty I once lost my room, but I got over it. Besides, never did I think Grammy might die in it or even worry about it. When did Jenni become so shallow?

"I have to call you back," was all I could muster through my building rage. Throwing the phone across the room, I wept until my throat became raw. The grief of feeling abandoned choked me.

"Families are supposed to support each other," I blubbered out loud, putting the pillow over my face to drown out the sound of my hysteria. "I've sacrificed everything for everyone my entire life. When do I get a little understanding and support?"

The phone rang.

I knew it was my good girl calling to apologize and make everything right, but I wasn't ready to answer. I was mad, and I wanted to stay mad, at least a little longer. The bee sting of my self-perceived betrayal would not ease, no matter how much baking soda I layered on.

The phone rang again, and I just stared at it.

Finally, knowing I had to face this conversation, I got up to call her back. But, just as I began to dial, the humanness of Jenni's concern slapped me hard. Death is creepy, and death is scary, especially for someone who has never had to deal with it.

"Oh my God." I began to cry again. "I never thought this part through. Maybe this is too much to ask of her, of all of them. This house will completely change with him here. Will they even want to come home again?"

No matter how much we redecorated, the knowledge that he had passed away would always stay with the room.

Picking up the phone, I dialed. "Jenni . . ."

"I'm so sorry, Mom," her sobs came. "Of course, he can have my room."

"No, honey. I'm sorry. I should have thought this through better," I tried to soothe. "I'm sorry for being upset. I know it's a gross thought that he might die in your room, but this is something I just have to do. I promise to make it up to you."

Hearing a calming to the convulsions on the other end of the phone, I explained my reasoning.

"Jenni, I love you. I know it feels weird and if he passes that way, you can have my room. But I can't watch him die in a hospital like your grandmother. I can't go through it again. Besides, I promised him and I have to see it through."

CHAPTER 6

Battling the Naysayers

Just when I thought I'd conquered everyone's fears about what would happen to my home and me if I gave up my life to care for my father, I needed to don my impenetrable shield of armor once more to battle an unsuspected naysayer.

"You can't be serious!" my gynecologist Patty exclaimed loudly. "You have no idea what you're getting yourself in for."

I lay naked on the examining table covered by a thin paper blanket, stunned at her outburst.

"What's the problem?" I asked, sorry that I even mentioned it as I noticed the expression in her eyes that read, You're crazy! "I've got everything ready," I proclaimed with confidence. "I can do this. Besides, how hard can it be? He's just an old man who sleeps all day."

Lifting up my arms, Patty sharply pressed two fingers into my armpit then started aggressively massaging my breasts, looking for lumps. By the narrowing of her blue eyes and her overzealous examination, I could tell I was in for a brutal schooling on self-preservation.

"Jackie, caring for an aging parent is very taxing. You need to put him in a home."

Frustrated that I was not being supported once again, I picked at the paper sheet covering my belly, feeling both physically and emotionally exposed and wishing I was anywhere but there. Having my entire face pricked with Botox, standing in a long line at the DMV, or going through another hip replacement would be far less torture.

"But that's the one thing I promised I'd never do. I have to keep my word."

Lifting up the mutilated paper sheet and placing my feet into stirrups as she opened my legs for a peek inside, she needled her gloved finger in, first to the right, then the left.

"Noticing anything unusual?" I asked, hoping to change the subject.

But knowing she now had a captive audience, she continued with her unsolicited advice.

"I'm just saying, you're not prepared for what's ahead. I wanted to do it for my parents and just couldn't. They had live-in help, but it all becomes just too much. There's a lovely facility in San Jose. I'll get you their information."

There it was again, that awful word: facility. Those sterile hospital-like settings for aging people who relied on overworked, underpaid, and often unavailable nurses to help them get dressed, use the bathroom, change sanitary undergarments, and wipe crystalized drool from their faces as they sat in a hallway all day with no one to talk to. A place with medicinal smells, loud noises, grumpy roommates, and boredom—my father's greatest fear.

Angrily, I kicked my feet out of the loops and sat straight up. Adjusting the crumpled, twisted paper cloth across my lap, I crossed my bare chest with my shivering arms, and declared, "I can do this. I will do this. He's not going to a nursing home."

Seeing she'd lost the battle—I can be pretty convincing when I allow my stubborn streak to prevail—Patty put her arms around me as if to say, I'm sorry. Instantly, I started to cry.

"Why is everyone so negative about my decision?" I wept. "It's not like I won't have help."

Blowing my nose into what became the largest Kleenex I'd ever used, I sat stark naked and explained to Patty how all this was going to work. I needed her on my side. Besides, weren't doctors supposed to want what was best for the patient?

"Look, we're keeping the caregiver he already has to help for a few hours during the day."

"I thought you said on your last visit that she was taking advantage of him by allowing a lot of people to stay in his house?"

"I know, but she can move him like no one I've ever seen. She needs the job badly, she doesn't charge much, and I'll be in and out all day to make sure there aren't any shenanigans going on. This will be an 8:30 to 4:00 p.m. job for her, going forward. I can easily handle the rest."

Feeling cold, I took the snotty, ripped coverlet and wrapped myself up again. I wanted out of there. I didn't need one more person telling me what to do.

"I've got this covered," I said boldly, proving I was Wonder Woman. "You'll see. Besides, he's ninety-five. How long does he have left?"

An hour later, I pulled into the driveway and stared at my home. It was about to undergo a makeover, but not a cosmetic one with lots of fresh paint and new furniture. Long ago, this structure housed sleeping babies who quickly became toddlers, rambunctious children, nasty teenagers, and, finally, charming adults. Our home was the place where my kids and all their friends came to hang out and where my family gathered for parties and the holidays. On top of it all, it was the only place since my childhood bed-room where I felt safe.

Was my life going to completely change? I contemplated as I sat in my driveway, staring at the blooming cherry tree in front of the living room window. Was I in complete denial? Christ, I felt like I did when I told my family I was marrying Dave. I remembered how no one could see the attraction, especially my mom. After all, he was three years younger, fresh out of college, not Catholic, and a Republican for God's sake.

Then, remembering how my marriage didn't turn out the way I wanted it to, I became worried the naysayers may be right.

Feeling a tear break loose as it slowly dripped down my cheek, my anxiety suddenly turned into rage.

"Damn you all!" I screamed over the sound of Rachel Platten's Fight Song on the car radio. "I'm going to show everyone—my brothers, my friends, and my kids!"

Wiping the blackened streaks away from my eyes, I decided no more tears. It was time to celebrate my last moments alone.

Entering the house, I went straight for the refrigerator. A glass of Rombauer Chardonnay always made me feel better, and I was going to enjoy every drop of the liquid gold, maybe the entire bottle. Dad would be here first thing in the morning and there was no turning back.

"Cheers, Dad!" I sang out, raising my glass to the corner where his chair would soon sit. "It's you and me until the end. We're going to do this, together."

The following day, I drove to San Carlos. Passing the oak

trees along Highway 280, I was reminded of all the years I'd made this half-hour trek. Looking at the Fitbit on my wrist that measured my footsteps each day, I began to wonder how many miles I had travelled to my parents' house over the past thirty years. If I added up all the get-togethers, holidays, parties, days of duty to clean their house, errand runs, visits to the various doctor appointments (senior citizens have a lot of those), and emergency trips to the hospital, I was sure my car had traveled across the country and back again at least fifty times.

I can't believe I won't be doing this anymore. I sighed. *It's been such a part of my daily routine. I wonder if I'll miss it.*

I thought back to when Michelle had just been born and how the time spent at my family home was fun. I loved watching both my mom and dad as they wrapped her in their arms as thoughts of the births of their own children took them back in time. Babies have a lovely way of not just adding new life to a home, but hope for the future too.

But after my grandmother moved in, Dad had his massive stroke, and Mom's health faltered in quick succession, the mood shifted south. Just as the short, bitingly cold days of winter bring a heaviness without the extra light, visits to my childhood home became unbearable as I listened to my mother moan, "This house is nothing but gloom and doom."

Staring through my windshield at my childhood home, I shook away the memories. Those were awful years. Mom was in such pain, and no matter what I did or how often I showed up, nothing made her happy. But while it was sad to think I was ending a chapter in my life, a new one was about to begin. I was determined to make it a happy ending, no matter how many people told me differently.

Bounding through the front door, I found Dad as I did every day, sitting by the same window my mother loved.

"Hi Dad," I called, but was quickly caught off guard by the image of him sitting alone, slumped in his chair, eyes closed.

When in the hell did he begin to look so old? I pondered, thinking that he didn't look that frail the day before.

Unlike my mother, whose age showed on every part of her body from the time she turned fifty, Dad maintained a youthful, handsome Spencer Tracey-like look: square jaw, rugged brow with deep-set lines that became engraved in his forehead from pensive thought over the years, furry caterpillar eyebrows that danced over his blue eyes when he laughed, and a dimple in his cheek that lit up his entire face when he smiled. Now, he was a shriveled shell of the man he used to be.

"Dad, are you ready?" I crooned, hoping to sound lighthearted as I touched his arm. "The movers will be here any minute to bring your bed and chair to my house."

Opening his eyes, he tried to focus on the tree outside the window. As always, little birds were flitting in and out, chasing each other just like his children once did on the lawn below.

"Your mother always loved those birds," he said wistfully.

"I know, Dad. I love them too." Sitting on the stool next to him, gently rubbing my hand over the dry skin on his sun-damaged arm, I tried to soothe him. "I have birds at my house too."

"I don't want to go."

Uh-oh! Here we go again.

"My refrigerator is filled with all the ice creams you like, every flavor."

"I changed my mind."

"I even made a batch of my famous chocolate cookies you love so much."

"I'm going to miss this house."

Feeling my body quiver, I was fearful tears would once again find their way to my tired eyes. Knowing I'd feel the same way when it was my turn to leave my home and memories, I was lost for words.

Maybe this is a mistake. Was I too rash to demand this?

But, knowing that he'd have issues with other caregivers if he stayed, plus the fact I'd have to be there every day to oversee things, I kissed his cheek and gently said, "I know, Dad. I'll miss this home too, but it's time. I promise you'll grow to love it at my house. I'll take good care of you."

Looking towards Enemi, I nodded with pleading eyes. Backing up and out of the way, I watched her lift my father with a count of one, two, three, and plop him into his wheelchair. Twirling him about, she turned and headed for the ramp. Quickly, his body shrank and his head became glued to his chest. Dad was withdrawing to his quiet space like he did when things became difficult. With a "do not disturb" sign draped over his presence, it was evident he was praying. He and God had some talking to do.

"You go on ahead," I called as she loaded him in his car. "I'm right behind you."

Walking through the house, emotions burned as if I were walking on hot coals, and I broke down.

"I want it back," I wept out loud, falling to the floor and clutching my knees to my chest. "I want those years when Mom danced through the house singing to show tunes as she cleaned. I want to watch Dad mow the lawn with the Giants game blaring in the background on his transistor radio. I miss hearing my brothers talking all at once and my grandmother telling stories of her time in silent movies. I miss my mom."

Knowing this was a piece of life long gone, I found myself wishing I could hide under my bed like I did as a child until all this sadness went away.

"Jackie, get a grip," I heard my consciousness speak. "Look at the bright side. At least you won't be driving up here on an instant's notice anymore to take him to the hospital. Doctors and hospital rides will begin and end at your home. There'll only be one house to keep clean, one refrigerator to fill, and less money spent on gas."

Giving my emotions a moment to swell and subside, I began to realize how truly tired I'd become after seven years of running back and forth on a daily basis.

I'm sorry, Dad, I prayed. *I know this is going to be hard for you. But I just can't do it anymore. I won't do it anymore. I've lost too much time.*

Wiping the deluge away from my face with my sleeve, I looked in the bathroom mirror to make sure mascara wasn't all over my face. I didn't want him to know I'd had a breakdown. Taking a deep breath, I stared at the sullen image looking back at me.

"You can do this, Jackie girl. You can do this."

When I pulled into the driveway a half hour later, Dad and Enemi were waiting patiently in the shade of a looming Redwood tree.

"I'm sorry it took me so long. There was a little accident," I fibbed. "Let me open the house. The ramp is on the patio."

Pushing open the gate, I ushered the two of them past the

garbage cans and around the corner of my well-manicured garden with white daisies, red American Beauty roses, and impatiens blooming in every color. And, just like at my parents' home on Windsor Drive, tiny birds sang in the trees as if to say, "Welcome, Jack. This is your new happy place."

"Won't this patio be nice to sit on? We can have lunch out here when the weather's warm."

With his head still down and eyes glued shut, I wondered if he was asleep.

"Dad, did you hear me?"

Silence.

"Dad?"

He held out his arm as if to say, "Cut it out." I stopped haranguing him and opened the door.

He'd be okay, I consoled myself. Just wait till he sees how much I spoil him. He'll wonder why he didn't move in sooner.

Once inside, Enemi wheeled him into his new bedroom.

"What do you think?"

Knowing he loved yellow and that his eyesight was fading, I had it painted it the most obnoxious, bright neon shade of butter.

"Dad? What do you think?" I asked again, hoping to get him out of his funk.

Finally opening his eyes, he lifted his head and looked around. Making a long, drawn out sigh, his acceptance was emerging. There was no turning back; he knew he had to make the best of things.

"I like the yellow. It makes the room cheery."

"I'm glad you like it. Where do you want me to put your bed?"

His eyes went directly to the window that looked out

onto a lovely maple tree, thick with emerald green leaves just beginning to uncurl and, once again, birds of various species darting in and out.

"Right there." He pointed. "I want to be able to look outside."

"Okay. Now let's look at where your recliner will go."

Grabbing the handles of his wheelchair, I thought it best that I start learning how to drive his mode of transportation. Enemi always held the keys, but she wouldn't be there 24/7. Backing him up, we got through the door, but when I turned him around, the footrest rammed the corner of the wall, taking out a chunk of painted drywall.

"Oops, sorry, Dad. Are you okay?" I feigned worry but felt annoyed that this might be just the first of many tragedies to my Benjamin Moore-painted walls.

Nodding, he waved it off as if swatting a fly. "Don't worry honey. She hit the walls all the time at home too. It just takes practice."

I'm going to have to be a lot more careful with my driving, or there'll be nothing left of my house.

Making it into the family room, I stood behind him, wrapped my arms around his neck, and pointed to the large picture window.

"And that's where your chair will sit. Won't it be great?" I heralded, happy with my decision. "You can look out the window, have fresh air anytime you want, plus be right in front of the TV for all your games."

"I don't like watching games."

This man adored his Giants and 49ers.

"Don't be silly. You love your teams."

"No, not anymore. Just turn on channel 229."

Scratching my head, I had no idea what could be so interesting on such an obscure station. Plus, I wasn't sure my TV would go back that far.

"What's on 229?"

"It's the Catholic channel. I want to go to Mass every day and say my rosary."

Being a man who never missed a day going to Mass, Dad found he could attend it by watching the service on TV. Maybe it wasn't as meaningful as kneeling in a pew, head bowed, as the priest conducted the sacrament, but it would do just the same.

Suddenly, the movers arrived.

"Great! Here comes your chair. We can get you settled while I fix up your bed."

Once the chair was put in place, Enemi yanked him out of his wheelchair and dumped him in it.

"Can I get you anything?" I asked before grabbing the sheets and blankets.

Shaking his head, he retreated again into his dark, quiet space for prayer. With his one good hand resting on his cheek, elbow firmly planted on the armrest, Dad went into seclusion and would remain there for the next five hours. Covering him with a blanket my mother had crocheted long ago, hoping that would make him feel a bit like home, I kissed him once again.

Okay, God! Please give me the strength, courage, and know-how to do this right!

CHAPTER 7

The Reality of Care

As our first day together wore on, quiet and uneventful, I found my thoughts cheering, See, I can do this! Caring for an old soul was no problem when all they did was sleep.

Standing in the doorway, watching his bowed head, closed eyes, and index finger resting just to the side of his nose—I smiled. Other than new surroundings, his life would be reminiscent of days recently gone by: prayerful, contemplative, and sedentary. The only break in his deep concentration would come when I asked if I could get him anything.

At 4:00 p.m., Enemi prepared for her departure, and my role as the gatekeeper was about to begin. Unfortunately, little did I realize that my duties as Florence Nightingale would entail more than delivering medications and fixing a Band-Aid or two.

"Okay, Jack," Enemi called, waking him from his peaceful trance. "Time to go to bed."

Nodding, he prepared himself to be lifted, thrown, and dropped one final time.

Watching with the intensity of a medical research analyst dissecting foreign particles under a microscope, I was determined to learn every aspect of his care. The last thing he needed was his daughter screwing up.

After extracting him from the recliner, Enemi wheeled Dad into his new room and parked him next to the bed. Next, she leaned over and locked the wheels for safety. Grabbing him by the transfer belt tied around his chest, she called out, "Okay, Jack! One, two, three." And, as if a magic fairy wand had been waved, he was catapulted to the edge of the bed. "Time to get ready for bed."

Gingerly lifting up his dead arm, she guided his blue golf shirt over the appendage and down his fingers. Gathering the fabric into continuous folds with her left hand, she pulled the garment over his head and slipped the remaining fabric off his right side.

Easy enough, I thought to myself, taking mental notes. *The pants should be no problem.*

Squatting to the floor, Enemi detached the Velcro strips of his black shoes and guided them off gently, exposing brown socks worn thin, his big toes playing peek-a-boo.

First order of business is to buy new socks.

Then came the brace and, finally, his gray sweat pants, which she yanked off with the speed and agility of a tablecloth being pulled out from under a place setting.

"What's next?" I asked.

"He won't be ready for dinner for a few hours," she responded. "But he needs his pants changed."

"You put another pair on him for bed? Won't he get hot?" I asked, perplexed. I knew how my father hated the feeling of being overheated.

"No, his diaper."

As if my mind were a car coming to a screeching halt to

avoid hitting the neighbor's dog in the middle of the road, my thoughts skidded to a halt.

Oh no! I forgot about this part.

For years, I helped my mother and grandmother with their "pants," a task that always made me queasy. But being that we had similar female body parts, I found a way to stomach it. Dad would be a different story.

"Right. How often does he need to be changed?"

"He'll need one more tonight and then again first thing in the morning."

I found myself wishing I was a little girl again and could hide in the fort Dave built in the backyard where no one would think to look for me.

"Jackie, did you hear me?" Enemi asked.

"Okay. Once more tonight and then in the morning. Gotcha!"

Knowing Dad would prefer some privacy during his unveiling, I left the room to clean up the mess left behind by a day filled with nothing.

Entering the family room, I was shocked to see the disarray. To make room for the manipulation of his wheelchair, Enemi had shoved all the other furniture out of the way. Carefully sliding the couch and coffee table back to their proper place, I repositioned the recliner. Looking down, I was horrified to already see tic-tac-toe scratch marks in my hardwood floor. Sighing, I closed my eyes. Between his wheelchair and her rearranging of furniture every day, I became fearful there'd be nothing left of my beautiful home.

God, help me let it go, I began to pray.

"Jackie, I'm leaving," Enemi called. "He'll want his dinner at 6:00 p.m., right after his rosary."

"Does he say his beads at an exact time every night?" I asked, walking her to her car.

"No, just turn on channel 229 at 5:30 p.m.," she informed me. "He prays with the nuns on TV."

"He prays with the nuns?"

"I think that's what you call them. Funny looking ladies covered in black from head to toe, mumbling the same words over and over." Rolling her eyes, she smirked and said, "Get ready. He needs the TV on full blast."

As I walked back into the house, memories returned from ten years before. In 2002, my parents' lovely home suffered an electrical surge during a violent storm that caused a blazing fire that ripped away the garage and caused smoke damage to the rest of the house. With no place to go, my parents stayed with me for three weeks until I could find a rental for them while the house was being rebuilt. Both were becoming hard of hearing, and every time the TV was on, the volume not only made our heads swim, but rattled the windows and walls.

Realizing my dad's visit was going to last a lot longer than three weeks, the thought of getting earplugs became very appealing.

Sitting with my 5:00 p.m. glass of wine, I watched the clock. A half hour later, I entered his room to start his evening prayers.

"Time for your rosary," I called, nudging him out of another meditative trance.

"Channel 229," he reminded me.

"I know, Dad, I know."

Flipping through the TV stations, I finally stopped on the

channel showing a room filled with ladies in head-to-toe black habits.

I'd thought the nuns got rid of those awful outfits years ago.

Twenty fresh-faced young women knelt onscreen, their faces peeking out from heavy headdresses—no make-up, no hair exposed, and every inch of skin hidden behind the thick black fabric. It looked like a scene out of the TV show, "The Flying Nun," and I wondered if a strong wind would send them flying too.

In the center of the mob sat a portly, beady-eyed woman they called Sister Angelica, who called out the prayers.

"Let's begin," her monotone voice announced. "Our Father . . ."

Knowing he was all set, I bent over and kissed his forehead.

"I'll be back with your dinner when it's over."

"Would you like to pray with me?" he shouted over the rumble of voices. If I didn't know better, I'd have thought they were a pack of yogis chanting om.

"Ah, thanks, Dad. Maybe some other night."

A half hour later, I was back. Turning off the TV, I sat next to him to spoon feed him chicken puree and mashed up vegetables. As he scarfed down each pulverized mouthful, I found it ironic that we turn into infants at the end of our lives, what between the baby food, the diapers, and the dependency.

And, just like in my childhood, no words were spoken as he devoured his food.

"Are you ready for some ice cream?"

Again, there was no conversation as he inhaled his favorte treat.

"Okay, Dad," I said, smiling. "What's next on the agenda?"

"My pills and then my teeth."

Counting the vast array of blue, yellow, pink, and gray tablets, I wasn't sure what any of them were for since the names of the vials were incomprehensible. Carefully dropping them into his mouth, I tentatively lifted a tall glass of cold water to his lips, careful not to spill.

"Thank you, honey. Now my toothbrush."

Fortunately, brushing his ancient pearly whites, which had become fossilized with the years, was one thing he could still do for himself.

Scrubbing away sideways, up, and down, he forced the brush with such intensity across his yellowed teeth and pink gums I was worried some of them might fall out.

"Okay," I declared, preparing myself for the final step to the evening. "I have to change your diaper now."

He shot me a glare, the same look I used to receive when I was caught feeding the family dog my dinner under the table as she sat at my feet.

"No! I'm fine. It can wait until the morning."

Oh no, I thought, terrified I was in for one of his moody, childish battles. *I guess he didn't get the memo that I'd be doing that part of his care too.*

"Dad, I have to change you. It's not healthy for you to lie in a wet diaper all night. You don't want to get a rash or bed sores, do you?" I added, appealing to his fear of pain.

While Dad was the strongest man I ever knew, the one thing he had an aversion to was pain. Any pain, whether it be a gaping wound or a minor sore throat, made him whimper.

"Couldn't we let it go just for tonight?"

"Oh, Dad," I giggled, trying to mask my fear. Slowly pulling back the blankets, I advised, "I know this is awkward for you, but just close your eyes and think of me as some cute nurse. This will be over in no time."

Pursing his lips, his expression shriveled like an apple doll left to dry in the hot sun for too long: body stiff, eyes shut tight.

Grabbing a fresh diaper from the tower of Depends next to his bed, I thought, How hard can this be? After all, I've changed a million poopy pants in my life.

But as I stood over his crippled body, a powerful avalanche of fear crashed down. This was no baby with a cute butt. This was my withered ninety-five-year-old father with a hairless groin and weenie shrunken to the size of a peanut. If this happened to all men, it was no wonder women lost interest in sex late in life.

What if it all goes bad? I worried. God knows I failed miserably changing Michelle's diapers when she first came home from the hospital. But, each time they fell off, my mom swooped into the rescue. Now I was all alone.

After detaching the plastic strips, I guided him onto his side and yanked off the soggy slab of paper pulp lined in plastic with no problem. Part two would prove to be a different story.

Shoving and yanking the dead weight of his body back and forth, I struggled to get the clean one positioned just right.

"Okay, Dad. Don't worry. I've got this," I feigned fearlessly.

Pushing him to one side, then the other, I rolled his body so many times I worried momentum might take over and he'd tumble off the bed. Several frustrating minutes later, I was sure I had it.

"All righty then. Let's see how this looks."

Rolling him over, I easily fastened the left side, but when

it came to the right, there was a gaping hole between the two ends and a vast expanse of white skin left exposed.

Oh my God! Now what do I do? There's no way I can do this all over again.

Sweat began dripping from the nearly five million pores in my body.

"Dad, I'll be right back!"

Totally flummoxed, I quickly ran to get the one piece of household equipment that always kept things together: the roll of electrical tape. Rushing back, my lifesaver in hand, I ripped a large piece of the gooey tape and secured the two ends together. Studying my handiwork, I caught Dad staring at me.

As my lip began to quiver, tears found their way down my cheeks.

"I'm so sorry. This will hold you together for now. I'll get it right tomorrow."

Grabbing my hand, he continued to look at me. Then, smiling sweetly, he said, "Honey, you're always so hard on yourself. You did just fine."

Kissing his check, I turned off the light and left to finish my meltdown in private.

Curling into a ball on the couch, I sobbed convulsively.

How could I be so stupid? I moaned. This wasn't how his first day was supposed to end. I was such an idiot.

But as I sat immersed in my pity party, I remembered the kind look on his face and the words that now hugged my heart: "You did just fine." Words I'd heard my entire life but were now rich in meaning. He believed in me. He always believed in me.

Dad, I promise I'll get all this right. You deserve the best, I said in my heart to his.

The following morning, as Enemi entered the house, I called

to her, "I need you to teach me how to do this." Coming into his room, she surveyed the crumpled mess and began to giggle.

"I can't let his happen again," I said, begging for help.

"Jackie, it isn't that hard." Obviously enjoying the fact she knew something I didn't, she told me her secret. "It's all about momentum."

"I tried that, but I was worried he'd go flying off the bed if I tried any harder."

"Let me show you now."

Fearful of being late for work, I implored, "Please, wait until I get home to do the last one. I want to watch. I'll be home before 4:00 p.m."

Later that afternoon, I flew into the house, ready for my tutorial. Although I had arrived at 3:45 p.m., I saw she had already finished her day's work.

"Enemi! I asked you to wait for me."

"I'm sorry, but he wanted to go to bed. You know your father. When he wants something, he wants it now."

Frightened of another debacle, I looked at him lying peacefully, eyes closed, off in prayer land.

Noticing the terror in my eyes, Enemi said sweetly, "I'll show you how I move his body without re-changing this one."

Grabbing another paper pad, Enemi brought it back to his bedside and tapped Dad's shoulder.

"Jack, we have to show Jackie how to do this correctly," she said loudly into his one good ear.

Opening his eyes, he shook his head no and demanded to be left alone.

"I don't want to do this again. I want to pray," he barked.

"Dad, you can stop praying for just one moment. You've been doing that all day," I pleaded. "This is important."

He grumbled in his annoyed manner when not getting his way, so I tried to reassure him, "We're not taking this one off. She's just showing me how to move your body so I don't mess it up like last night."

"Make it quick!"

When she placed her hands under his back and lifted him slightly, Dad took the one arm that still functioned and grabbed the opposite railing of the hospital bed. Pushing him up even higher, she quickly threw the new diaper under his bottom and rolled him back, both tabs in their precise location for easy fastening.

"See, it's as easy as that."

"That's what I tried to do last night. Can you do it again?"

Enemi did a replay, and now two diapers were perfectly in place. Looking at the stack below his bottom, a miraculous thought crossed my mind.

Wondering if he was stuck in this prone position, I asked Enemi, "He doesn't roll around, does he?"

"No," she answered, confused. "He stays right there the whole night."

"Yes!" I cried. "I've got the greatest idea."

It's been said that necessity is the mother of invention, and this mother just created a doozy.

"Don't take those away. I can get the old one off. I just can't get a new one on."

Looking at my dad with two clean diapers perfectly poised under his bottom, my life was saved. Like in the story of The Princess and the Pea where the princess slept on several mattresses, my dad would be my slumbering prince piled high on a mountain of Depends.

"When you prepare him at night, I want you to place three to four more diapers underneath him. That way if I have to change him more than once, there won't be any issues."

Leaning over, I kissed him on the cheek, and happily announced, "Dad, we've got you covered now! No more mistakes on my end."

"I'm sorry I'm such a bother," he mumbled, glistening tears forming in the corners of his eyes. "This is all too much for you."

Stunned that these words had come out of his mouth, I stopped in my tracks, my "Eureka!" moment fizzling.

"No, no!" I declared, moving my face close to the face of the first man who ever loved me. "We're good. Please don't feel like that. I can do this!"

The magnitude of where his life had been and what it had become was now overwhelmingly visible. Dad was a man who'd lost everything—first his mobility, then his wife, his driver's license, home, eyesight, hearing, and the ability to do his finances. Now, his daughter had to change his pants. It was sort of okay when someone else did it; after all, they got paid. But it was a different story when his daughter had to take on the task.

"Dad, I'm so happy to be able to do this for you."

Seeing the sadness wash over his eyes, I whispered in his ear before kissing his cheek, "I never want to hear you say that again. All we needed was a little practice."

Patting his wrinkled cheek, it was time for the next item on the list of things to do. "Let's turn on channel 229. Ready for your rosary?"

CHAPTER 8

Selling the Family Home

A week later, on July 8th, I found Dad slurping his maple-flavored Quaker oatmeal with Enemi's help. Looking up, he smacked his lips and announced with certainty, "It's time to sell the house and I want you to do it."

A listing is the one thing every realtor goes cuckoo for Coco Puffs for. In the industry, realtors have a motto for longevity: "You need to list to last." And while I was no different than any other agent, salivating at the idea of my name being plastered all over a signpost, I was having a hard time comprehending why my dad needed to sell now.

"But Dad, you just moved in here. We can wait. What if you decide you don't want to live with me anymore? Then what?"

With his bushy eyebrows creeping downward, nearly covering his eyes, he opened his mouth and accepted another spoonful of the mushy mess. "Do it," he restated.

"Dad, are you sure?"

As with any situation, when my father said his piece and didn't want to be challenged any further, a wall of silence rose. Then, in a tone barely above a whisper, I heard him say, "I want a nice family in there."

Driving to work, I thought how strange this was going to

be. For fifty-two years, 112 Windsor Drive had been our family home. It was the one place that remained constant in my life: my sanctuary, my refuge from the cruel world outside, and my safe house when I found myself grappling with self-esteem.

"This is too soon," I said to myself, looking into the rearview mirror and applying an extra coat of mascara while sitting at a stoplight. "I think he's being rash."

But, knowing my dad never did anything rashly—in fact, every decision he ever made came from long hours of deliberation and prayer—I decided to drive to San Carlos and take a look at what preparing the house for market would entail. I knew there was a lot of stuff. As products of the Great Depression, my parents stored away every rubber band, paperclip, plastic tie wrap, and piece of tin foil, all waiting to rise again like a phoenix from the ashes, to be more useful than before.

A half hour later, pulling into the driveway, I sat for a moment staring at our home in all its avocado puke-green glory.

I wondered if there was enough money in the budget to paint the entire house?

For reasons I never understood, my mother loved that color and bathed the house in it—inside and out. She even used it as her signature color in just about every outfit she wore.

Walking up the path to the front door, I was pleased to see the gardener was still doing his job. The Boxwood hedging had recently been trimmed, forming a perfect border under my mother's bay window. The Chinese Maple was in full bloom, and tiny multi-colored impatiens grew in a massive cluster underneath.

Climbing the pink sandstone steps, I was reminded of all the years I flew up them two at a time, throwing the door open to announce, "I'm home!" But walking in today, I was overcome by a dispirited feeling. While things were just as we left them in their perfectly appointed places, the house felt bitterly cold, even on this hot July day. It was empty of human warmth, and the silence screamed, "Nobody lives here anymore."

"Okay, girlfriend," I said to myself, feeling the need for a little company. "Put on your realtor hat. This is no time for emotion. You have a big job to do, so let's get it done."

Our home was your typical ranch-style, 2,300-square-foot building with four bedrooms and two baths. There was a formal living and dining room, family room and kitchen combo, and a small laundry room down the hall. In the two-car garage, cabinetry lined the walls and on every shelf, stuff had been stored. Wondering what room would be the least emotional to clear out first, I went straight for the kitchen.

"Remember, most of this is junk," I said out loud. "Create piles: save, give away, and throw away. Just like all your other listings, if you follow the pattern, you'll get through this with ease."

In my youth, the kitchen had been my favorite room in the house, and not just for the obvious reason of food. It was where our family gathered for dinner and talked about our day. It was also where I began to grow close to my mother in junior high while she'd prepare the evening meal. Up until that point, we were mother and daughter, but not friends. She was always busy keeping order in our crazy home, and I was content to stay in my room and play with my dolls, hiding from the carnage my brothers were creating. But, when puberty hit, I Velcroed my body to the only vessel of female hormones in the house.

Two women were better than one, especially when up against an army of four—my three brothers and father.

Sitting on the counter, watching her chop, we'd find time for girl talk with no interruptions from the male species. There we discussed makeup, the latest fashions, even sex.

"Mom, Mary said she saw two kids over in the creek naked," I huffed and puffed one late afternoon in the seventh grade. Sex Ed had yet to be a staple in the school curriculum, and I was a bit of a late bloomer in body and knowledge.

Putting her knife down, my mother turned to look at me, eyes wide. "Really?"

"Yeah! She said they were having sex and that he was sticking his thingy inside here," I fumed, pointing to my own underdeveloped woman parts. "Isn't that disgusting?"

I could tell by the look on her face and her pause that something about what I had said was leaving her speechless, and my mother was never speechless. Confused by her lack of response, I continued on. "That's not how it happens, is it?"

She pushed the knife further away on the counter, her face turning as red as her apron. Shifting her body weight from one foot to another, she stalled.

"Mom?"

Moving in close for this most intimate of all mother-daughter conversations, she cupped my innocent face in her hands and said, "Yes, honey. That's how it happens."

"No! Really? That's gross."

A twisted smile appeared on her face as her hands now steadied themselves on my knees.

"Don't tell me you and Dad do that?" I blurted before she could give me some God fearing version of the birds and the bees.

Kissing my cheek to calm me down, the only words she could muster were, "Yes."

Instantly, I wanted to go run and hide under my bed and pretend we had never had this conversation.

"God! It all sounds disgusting!" I screamed. Positive the only reason to copulate was to have babies, I asked, "So you and Dad did it four times? Then I'm only having one kid."

Standing in the middle of the kitchen more than fifty years later, remembering the moment as if it were yesterday, I began to laugh hysterically. Years later I'd grown to understand the joy in sex and, just like my mother, I did it four times, plus a lot more.

But, just as quickly as I had giggled, I instantly became saddened as I opened the kitchen cupboards. The food I loved as a kid had vanished. Instead of Oreo cookies, Tostitos Corn Chips, Fruit Loops, or Kilpatrick bread, several boxes of oatmeal sat in their place, along with rows and rows of canned peaches, pears, and pineapple.

Turning to the shelves below, I was shocked to find enough plastic to fill a recycling center. Tucked away were twenty Cool Whip containers, thirty Tupperware canisters of all shapes and sizes, at least fifteen I Can't Believe it's not Butter buckets, and too many cottage cheese tubs to try to count. They were all missing lids.

There were enough containers in here to store two Thanksgiving dinners. Why did they save all this?

But remembering a village once lived here too, it made sense.

Next came the shelves filled with chipped plates and saucers that were no longer a set, Libbey glassware fogged up from too many showers through the dishwasher, bud vases with the necks broken off, and one coffee cup. Having done this before for other clients, I created a staging center on the kitchen table for what would be kept or thrown away. Sadly, all this would be thrown out.

Then came the pots and pans and, finally, the refrigerator.

Opening the double doors, the reality made my heart sink.

"Oh my!" I sighed out loud. "Smells like someone died in here. I don't need just a pair of gloves, I need a HAZMAT suit to clear this all out."

In the corner, a half-eaten chicken was now showing signs of petrification. More little containers were scattered on each shelf, housing a spoonful of moldy peas, a dollop of scalloped potatoes covered in a green film, and canned fruit complete with spores swimming on top of the juice, all with dates written on pieces of masking tape dating back two months. Dad had only been living with me a little over a week and these leftovers had expired long before.

Closing the doors quickly, knowing I'd need a pile of cleaning supplies to handle the job, I decided I'd tackle the fridge at a later date. This was going to take time, thought, patience, and a nose plug.

Two hours later, I returned home to find my dad in his chair, maintaining his daily position, mind wandering elsewhere behind closed eyes.

"Hi Dad," I called, approaching his recliner. "I'm back."

Instantly, he opened his eyes, smiled, and asked, "Did you sell the house already?"

Knowing this wasn't just some silly question but a moment of his dry wit, I kissed his cheek and chuckled. "I need a little more time. You have a lot of stuff in there."

"Wait till you see the garage."

"Oh, great!" I giggled. "Thanks for the heads up."

"Your mother just couldn't give anything away."

Rubbing his eyes, Dad wiggled his stiff body attempting to get comfortable, then asked, "How long do you think you need to get it ready?"

Sitting on the edge of the coffee table, I came up with a timeline. Despite the fact my father's body had abandoned him, his mind was still sharp. This was his home and he deserved to be involved in the process and have a say in how things went.

"You have a lot of stuff I need to clean out. Is there anything special you want me to keep?"

I could see by the look in his eyes he was perusing every room, remembering what was left behind.

"I don't need anything, but I want you children to divide up what you'd like. The one thing I do want is for my books to have a new home."

My father had a passion for the written word. I often wondered if he licked the ink right off the page as he devoured a book a week. There was not a day in his adult life that at some point, a novel wasn't in his hands. As his world became limited in those years after my mom's passing, he spent his time eating, napping, and reading. He read so much that his stack of books reached half way to the ceiling on the fireplace hearth, and that didn't count the other pile next to his bed.

"That's a lot of books. Even if we divided them by four, I doubt any of us could read them all."

"One day you will. What do you think we should price the house at?"

Smiling, I realized that despite his world of memories,

he was still interested in the bottom line and the almighty dollar.

"I'm not sure yet. It's going to take me a couple of months to get it ready. I have to find places for all your things, then paint, carpet, and stage. It's July so I hope to have it ready by the middle of September."

With a nod of his head, we were in agreement. For the next two and half months, I put my head down and focused. There'd be no room, or time, for emotions. I had a job to do.

The following day, well-equipped with boxes, bags, and cleaning supplies, ready to tackle the dreaded refrigerator, I showed up at 9:00 a.m.

"Okay," I announced, opening the doors again. "Get ready, old food. You're out of here."

Looking at the freezer first, I saw that there was enough food to feed an entire nation. The only problem was it now had frostbite. Dumping it all into the plastic bags, I heard my mom yelling at me, "That's wasteful! And waste is a sin."

Sorry, Mom. But this has got to go.

Next, donning gloves up to my elbows, I took my arm and swept each shelf of the fridge into more bags: all the dishes, containers, cans, and tin-foiled-wrapped-somethings I was afraid to open. Seven bags and an hour later, off to the garbage can it all went.

"Okay, that's done," I announced, proud of my accomplishment. "Where to next?"

Because my energy was waning, I decided my room would be easy to tackle. After my grandmother left for the nursing home, my mother decided to move in and give my father a break from all her moaning and groaning during the night. Shortly after she passed away, I cleared out all her belongings as well. I expected a fairly clean slate, but I was horrified when I opened the door. While it had seen its fair share of use after I moved out, Enemi had completely destroyed it when she moved in.

"My beautiful furniture!" I screamed. "What was she doing in here?"

On the tops of my dresser and desk, evidence of spilled nail polish smeared the varnish with various shades of red, purple, and blue. A thick layer of dust, looking like gray snow, coated the furniture, and the white rug was covered with food stains.

"Even the curtains are ruined! How does someone wreck curtains?" I said, aghast.

The frilly white shades that once framed the window to the world beyond were now tilting sideways and hanging in shreds.

"Did she have a wild cat in here?"

Gripping my fingers into a tight fist, anger began rising to the surface. I had to let it go. Again, this was no time for tears.

Two hours later, the drawers were empty of debris and the closets were cleared of paper bags, shoeboxes, wire hangers, mismatched socks, and a few forgotten undergarments. My curtains were taken down and the furniture wiped off as three more trash bags were added to the pile outside.

As the days and weeks blended one into another, every day the routine was the same. I meticulously went through each drawer and box, opened every book to make sure no money was hidden inside (my mother had a habit of saving for a rainy day in secret places), and systematically found homes for fifty-two years of stuff. It was exhausting and led me to not just a glass of wine at night, but the entire bottle.

But one day, while clearing out Dad's office filled with tax returns dating back to the 1950s, I discovered a treasure.

There at the bottom of the pile rested a tiny envelope addressed to my mother: a note from him dated on their wedding day.

Dear Lassie, You're the only girl I love, the only girl I ever loved and will ever love.

Stunned to see his handwriting on this small card, I knew it must have come with his wedding gift to her, a string of pearls that I now treasured. Instantly, I became misty eyed.

"How sweet is this? Thank God I didn't just throw stuff out. I wonder if there are other letters hiding."

This brought new commitment to comb through things carefully, adding several more weeks to the already laborious routine. And, with each new purging came priceless treasures: pictures I'd never seen before, love letters from Dad to Mom, and the script from the play "White Cargo" my grandfather won awards for acting in.

Finally, the day came—time to get it ready for market.

"Okay! Let's get this puppy painted, staged, and carpeted!"

In just two weeks, the house was transformed into a beautiful showcase. Floors once hugged in green carpet became a sea of realtor beige, complemented by neutral colors covering the walls. All our personal photos and knick-knacks were removed, and in their places sat contemporary Pottery Barn furniture.

The home lasted on the MLS for two days before we received three offers. As expected, my father gave the home to a young Catholic couple that did not make the highest offer, but were about to start their family with the promise of sending their children to St. Charles, just as he had.

"So, are you happy?" I asked two days before escrow closed. A whopping check of $950,000 was about to be put in his bank account. "Not only did we do better than expected, but I know they will love the home just as much as we did."

Smiling from ear to ear, he nodded. "I'm very pleased." Then, he said the unexpected.

"I'd like to see it again."

CHAPTER 9

Time to Say Goodbye

Surprised that he wanted to see his home again, I suddenly became worried. It didn't look like the house he remembered.

"Why do you want to see it?" I asked, hoping to make it sound like a bad idea. "It's such a long drive and you know how tired you get sitting in the car."

Looking into my eyes, his face softened. I could see by the gentle expression this was important.

"I want to say goodbye."

Thinking of past clients who'd sold their homes of forty or fifty years and returned to them one last time, I knew most left saddened by the experience. Scared it might upset him, I asked again, "Are you sure? It doesn't look the same."

"Please."

The following day, Enemi loaded him up in her car, wheelchair safely tucked away in the trunk, and off they went as I drove behind. I knew I'd have my own goodbyes to say and wanted to do them alone. Up to that point there'd been no real tears. But, like with any true grieving process, not only did I know they would come, but I wanted to do justice by them.

Pulling up behind, I saw that Enemi had parked inside the garage where I'd had a wheelchair ramp installed three years before, once it became clear he couldn't manage the stairs.

I took the spot on the street.

"Okay, Dad. Let's get you inside," I said as I met them.

Maneuvering up the ramp, first into the laundry room and then around the narrow corners of the hallway, we headed straight for the living room. With his chin resting on his chest, I allowed my fears to diminish when I remembered his vision had deteriorated. Maybe he wouldn't truly see how much the house changed.

Enemi smiled at the changes, while my father's gaze went straight to the light from the window as it danced on the floor.

"How your mother loved that bay window," he said finally, with just a hint of a smile.

Rubbing his back, I agreed, "Yes, Dad. That was the best addition to this house you ever made. I remember how she used to love to lie on the couch and look out."

Again, silence. With a job to get back to and an escrow to close, I needed to get a move on. After a few minutes, I asked, "Are you ready to see the rest of the house?"

With his nod, we turned to travel down the hallway, past the bedrooms where his four children once slept, and finally into the master suite that he shared with his wife for over half a century: his sanctuary where, like his daughter, he too hid from the world when it became stressful or unkind.

He looked around the room from one side to the other without saying a word. This room held the most memories for him, for it was within these walls he and my mother connected both verbally and physically. By the look on his face, I sensed he was pleased with being home once again. It was the same look he gave me every time I walked into the room to spend some time with him.

Turning in my direction, he reached out his hand to grab mine and with a tender squeeze, he asked, "Can I see the rest of it?"

"Of course, Dad. Let's go."

He quietly nodded as we passed each room again.

"What are you thinking about?" I asked, wondering what was going on in his quiet mind.

"Just how I used to love watching you kids sleep. I could stand there all night as you dreamed away."

Smiling, I found myself remembering the nights I couldn't fall asleep and became aware of his head peeking in on me. When I was in the sixth grade, I developed a nasty case of insomnia. Fearful of flunking my subjects, I'd lie awake for hours staring at the ceiling.

Knowing I was struggling, he'd often come in, sit on my bed, and pat my arm. First, we'd talk about whatever test I was about to take, then he'd hand me my rosary. "Hold it close," he would say. "It will take your fears away."

Finally, we reached the family room and kitchen. By now, I was becoming antsy. I needed some input as to what he thought; was he upset or did he like what I'd done to the place? I knew he was happy with the price because he received $50,000 more than expected. I couldn't wait any longer and broke the silence.

"Dad, what do you think of the staging?"

"I can't see it, honey, but it looks great. You did a wonderful job." Then, he took a huge breath, let it out slowly, and said, "Okay, it's time to go home."

"But, Dad, this is your home," I quickly responded, forgetting we'd just sold it.

Looking up as he reached for my hand again, he smiled that sweet Irish grin that always melted my heart.

"Sweetie, it now belongs to someone else. My home is with you."

As we turned to wheel him out, I began to realize why it was so important for him to come back. He wanted to visualize our life together one last time, as if it were a memory box filled with precious items from a time long ago. But now, there'd be no turning back. Like everything else that was taken away from him, he would surrender this to God too. For better or worse, he was now stuck with me until the end.

"Okay," I answered, hugging his neck. "Time to go home. It's you and me forever."

"Will you be right behind?" he asked.

"I'll be home in a bit. I need to do a few things here."

Waving goodbye with the promise to be home soon, I sat on the floor of my empty bedroom. Now clear of the stained rug, my furniture, and curtains, I stared out the window at the willow tree that had grown massive with the years.

I had grown up with that tree. Watching it bend with the wind, I used to make up stories in my head about how my life would one day look. I wanted ten kids and a husband who adored me.

Feeling a tear sliver its way down my cheek, I was reminded that while the husband part didn't work out, I did have four wonderful children.

Looking around, memories of the years between those walls flooded my mind. I remembered the dollhouse that stood in one corner and the nursery for my menagerie of baby dolls in the other. As I grew up and the toys found their way to the attic, they were replaced with a vanity for applying makeup and a rocking chair for sitting in as I devoured the latest romance novel. It was also where my mother gave me one of the most precious gifts, the first of many journals complete with a gold key to keep prying eyes out. In those pages, I spewed my innermost thoughts, fears, and dreams.

Suddenly, the dam burst. The little Dutch boy could no longer plug the hole as my tears gushed.

"God, I hate all this!" I screamed, wanting to go back to the days when I rode my bike freely around town, climbed the trees across the street, and played with my dolls. "I don't like being the grown-up."

As my emotions fumed, I became angry that no one had prepared me for this part of my life. Sure, I knew my parents would eventually grow old and die, but there were no classes on how to accept that one day, homes would be gone and that parents would need to be raised by their children.

"I'm so tired of being alone all the time," I moaned. "Every decision I make, I have to do by myself. Even caring for him—it's all left up to me."

In my tired mind, I wrangled over the unfairness of my life: that my husband left me right in the middle of raising teenagers, that my two responsible brothers lived several hours away making it difficult for them to be on call at a moment's whim, that my local brother was dealing with his own personal issues and could not be relied upon for any kind of help, and that my children had grown up and discovered lives of their own. I was lonely. I was sad. I felt put upon. I was also angry—very angry.

"I don't want to be responsible anymore. When will someone finally take care of me?"

Letting the emotion get the best of me, I sat for several minutes in the quiet of my special place. Finally, I gathered myself, wiped away the melted mascara that covered my cheeks, and blew my nose into the sleeve of my sweatshirt. It was time to say goodbye to the soul of our family.

It was in this house where we clung to each other in hard times and hugged joyously in the good. Our front door was never locked and welcomed anyone and everyone. But, more importantly, 112 Windsor Drive was the scrapbook that held all my family's memories on our journey of love and learning.

But Dad was right; it was time to release its heart into the loving arms of a new family so their children would grow up loving, Catholic, and strong, just as we had. And, like so many things in my life, I would rely on my father's art of surrender to get me through.

CHAPTER 10

Conversations in the Dark

Crawling into bed two nights later after a long and particularly exhausting day dealing with an angry seller who wanted to cut my commission because her piece-of-shit house wasn't speaking to a buyer, my tired body just wanted to shut off my brain. Reaching for an Ambien and a soothing glass of Cabernet, a habit for sleep I was becoming dangerously accustomed to, I crawled into bed. Pill and glass in hand, I heard a blood-curdling scream from down the hall.

"Jackie! Jackie!"

Crap!

Spilling most of the wine on my white comforter, I placed the glass on the nightstand along with its best friend for sleep, the tiny pink pill.

"Dad, I'm coming," I called, jumping out of bed.

"Jackie!"

"I'm coming, Dad!"

While I was always Johnny on the Spot when it came to my kids' cries in the night, at least I knew they could get out of bed on their own. Dad was a different story. I raced down the hallway as he continued to scream.

"Jackie!"

"Dad, I'm coming!"

Racing even faster, I'd forgotten that I'd polished the wooden floors that day. Just as I was about to turn the corner, my stockinged feet went out from under me. I slammed into the wall, knocking the photos of my kids through the years off their hooks.

I found myself on the floor in the middle of toothless grins and broken glass.

"Holy Mother of God," I uttered with a surly grunt.

"Jackie! Are you coming?"

"Dad, I'm right here," I yelled, pulling myself up.

Tiptoeing through the minefield of shattered glass, I entered his room to find my father just as I'd left him several hours earlier: on his back, staring up at the ceiling, rosary in hands. He hadn't moved, let alone fallen to the floor, and there were no remnants of his boiled chicken dinner regurgitated on his chest, a reflux that occasionally happened.

"Are you okay?" I said nervously, fighting to keep my voice steady. Reaching his side, I stared down at him. Nothing seemed amiss.

He gave me that quick boyish grin of his and asked, "Want to chat?"

Do I want to chat? What the hell! I thought you were dying!

But looking into his happy eyes, I took a breath, letting the irritation melt from my face. "Sure, Dad. What do you want to talk about?"

Growing up, my father never talked about his life or anything else for that matter. I always assumed it was because he was tired all the time. And who wouldn't be? He was out the door at 6:00 a.m. for his hour-long train ride to San Francisco every day. Next, he'd go to Mass (there wasn't a day that he missed the sacrament), then to his job as an appellate conferee for the Internal Revenue Service, where he'd sit at his desk pouring over numbers and the law, contacting taxpayers trying to make amends with the government. He never left for lunch but carried in his pocket a bagged sandwich that he prepared for himself.

Twelve hours later, he walked back in the door, sat down for dinner with the family, and gobbled his food at such fierce speed I often wondered if he were afraid someone would take it away from him. Immediately after dinner, he melted into his supple red leather chair along with the newspaper and his pipe. In all the years I lived at home, there was never any variation to his routine.

On the weekends, he wasn't like the other fathers who spent their free time in front of the TV watching baseball or football, beer (or two) firmly in hand. Instead, he spent his days off washing the windows, scrubbing the bathrooms, and doing the yard work. On Sunday, for good measure, he polished four tiny pairs of uniform shoes so we'd look our best on Monday mornings at school. While he loved his Giants and the 49ers, sitting in front of the boob tube was considered a sacrilege, a complete waste of time. Instead, his transistor radio followed him wherever he went.

"Does Dad ever talk to you?" I often asked my mother when I was as a child and a teenager.

"Of course he does, silly. Why do you ask that?"

"Well, it just feels like you're the one who does all the talking. He just sits there."

Since my mother was the extrovert, I often wondered if Dad

just left the entertaining and disciplining of the children to her knowing he'd never get a word in edgewise. Why waste the effort when you could be zoning out? It wouldn't be until he moved into my home and we had late night chats about the past that I truly glimpsed the man he was.

"Okay, what would you like to discuss?" I asked, picking slivers of glass off my flannel nightgown.

"I don't know, you choose."

Looking at his appreciative smile, my heart melted. He could be so sweet sometimes.

"Dad, you must have something on your mind. You called me in here."

Taking my hand, he sat for a moment in silence still smiling. Then squeezed it, and said, "I was just lying here and realized I missed you."

Wanting to throw my arms around him, I kissed his cheek instead. Maybe this is why you're living with me. So I can finally know and understand the man you are.

"I'm right here. Let's talk."

For the next two hours, we discussed my work life and how I could be more assertive with my clients. Because I was constantly a peacemaker, it left room for those who liked to take advantage to walk all over me.

"You just have to stand up and say no," he instructed, his tone casual.

"Easy for you to say. Men were born saying that word."

My father always had a quiet dignity when he spoke. There were never superlatives, other than "that's terrific," and no flowery wording. Just straight to the point.

"You don't give yourself enough credit. You are a strong

woman who has accomplished a lot. Just look at all you've done since Dave left. You raised four kids by yourself and reinvented your life in the workplace. You've even held onto two houses when other women would be forced into a rental."

Taking a moment for a breath, he put his hand over his heart and patted it twice. "Trust yourself as you learn to set some boundaries, and you'll be just fine."

Next, we went over each of his four grandchildren and what they were doing with their lives. We dissected the recent political nature of the world and discussed if Barack Obama would be chosen for another term. As a die-hard Democrat, Dad was of the opinion that Republicans needed to stay locked out.

We covered a lot of ground, and just when I thought there was nothing more to say, I remembered a photograph I found earlier that day, hidden in an old book from his childhood that he'd kept all these years.

"Dad, I found a picture of you today. On the back, it says you were fifteen."

With eyes wide, he exclaimed, "You did! What was I doing in it?"

"You were standing with a football and a boy named Lloyd."

A pause came over the room. Then, softly, my father said, "Lloyd was my best friend for years."

In the sepia photograph, my father stood in dirty slacks, a dress shirt, and a pullover sweater looking like he had been heading for church but, with the football in hand, had taken a detour. Next to him, a boy a few inches taller stood with a dark mop of hair sticking straight up and deep-set, Italian-looking eyes peering above a blanket he had wrapped around himself. On the back, my grandmother had written, "Jack at 15 with his best chum, Lloyd." Unlike my mother, whose father had taken up photography as a hobby and chronicled her life from birth until his death, there were very few pictures of anyone on the Madden side of the lineage.

"Really? Tell me about him."

Searching his memory, Dad stared at the ceiling.

"We were very close for a long, long time. But one day I got mad at him. We were playing ball, and I thought he was cheating, so I grabbed my football and went home."

"Really? Did you two make up?"

Playing with the top of the sheet with his gnarled fingers, I could see the curtain coming down over his face. This was a painful piece of his past.

"Dad?"

"I wasn't very nice. He tried to apologize, many times, but I never accepted it. And I've regretted it my whole life."

Untangling the sheet from between his fingers, I held his hand once again.

"Dad, you were just a kid. Kids do things like that. I'm sure you feel bad now but know this—when you get to heaven, Lloyd will be there waiting."

"You think so?"

"Absolutely! I believe heaven is a place of pure love. You've even said this yourself. This crazy stuff we put ourselves through will no longer exist and it will only be souls. All this nonsense we do in our human form will be left behind."

For a while, we sat in the quiet of the dark night. Just a father and daughter holding each other's hands. As I thought he was about to drift off, he opened his eyes and asked, "Does Michelle have any boyfriends?"

Where is that coming from?

"No, Dad. She doesn't."

"How about Jenni?"

"Nope, not Jenni either. The only one in our family seeing anyone is Lauren. Remember? His name is JJ."

"Oh yeah, Joe Joe."

"No, Dad. It's JJ."

"JJ, Joe Joe, what's the difference?" he said with a wink.

"Dad, that is so silly. Do you plan on messing up the name of the first guy who wants to seriously date me?"

Suddenly, an unexpected sternness glossed over his eyes, much like the look he had given me when I crashed the back of the station wagon into a telephone pole when I was sixteen.

"I'm sorry, but you're done. No more dating for you."

Huh?

"Dad, how can you say that?"

"Well, it wasn't your fault, but you only get one chance. Look at me. After your mother passed away, I wasn't interested in anyone else."

It had been eight years since my mother left us and he was now ninety-five. The thought of my father eyeing other women was a bit unsettling, but I was still young enough to get my legs up.

Knowing this was all coming from his Catholic training— that you marry once and for life, no divorce—there was no point in arguing. It was a conversation I was sure to lose.

"Let's talk about women you dated before Mom," I said, thinking most likely there were none, but at least it would get us off the topic of me. "I bet you were shy with the girls."

Despite the fact my dad was very handsome, I always thought he would have been rather awkward as a young man with the ladies. He was quiet, reserved, proper, and lived with his parents until he married Mom at twenty-nine. Bringing a girl home for a roll in the hay, or even a cup of tea, would have been embarrassing for him.

"Did you do much dating before you got married?" I asked, sure of the answer.

With absolutely no humility or a moment to even think about it, he announced proudly, "I was a catch back then. All the girls wanted to date me."

Whoa Nelly! I wasn't expecting that!

"There was a nurse I went out with for a while," he continued. "She was pretty, but she wanted to get married and I didn't."

Watching his face light up, I couldn't help but giggle. He was a stud, and he knew it.

"Really? How did you handle that?"

Laughing raucously, he ran his hand through his thick white mane. "I got lucky. The war came along."

"What?"

"Yeah, I went into the Navy and never saw her again. I dodged that one."

We both broke down in hysterics: him at the ease of getting out of a sticky situation and me over the thought that war was the perfect solution.

"Nice one, Dad."

Squinting, utterly pleased with himself, he continued, "Everyone wanted to marry me."

"But Mom was the one who caught your eye."

I could tell he was remembering the image of my exquisite mother. In her youth, Lassie was breathtakingly beautiful with her auburn-red hair, saucer-like blue eyes, Barbie doll figure, and gregarious personality. Despite the fact that she never performed in Hollywood like her parents, her magnetic persona filled any room she walked into. Her exquisite features always mesmerized me. I could only imagine how my father must have felt.

"Your mother was something," he said smiling, his eyes now dancing. "Like a firecracker, she constantly exploded, but it was a joyful type of combustion. When I went off to war, I prayed she'd wait for me."

"It must have made you so happy to come home and know she was still there."

"I knew I had to snag her quickly before someone else did."

"That's sweet, Dad. I love hearing these stories."

As he began to yawn and close his eyes, I found myself feeling grateful for this time we had together. We had never had these types of conversations before.

The days could be long and having Enemi in the house was annoying for I was used to being alone and all she did was lay around the house once my dad was in his chair. But I planned to take any opportunity I was given for more moments like this, even if they were in the middle of the night.

"Are you getting sleepy?"

With an affirmative nod, he closed his eyes, and I covered him up, kissed his cheek one last time and told him I loved him. Then I I turned on his favorite CD of classical music with angelic singing in the background. It was a meditative CD I one day found at the music store that calmed the nerves and seem to speak to his soul.

"I love you too, sweetie. Can we talk some more tomorrow?"

"Yes, Dad. Tomorrow and every day."

CHAPTER 11

Doctor Appointments

Two months passed since our midnight chat. We were tiptoeing into November and life was speeding by at an alarming pace. I almost wondered if our hourglass had an extra-large hole, causing the sand to pour rather than fall grain by grain. The hours seemed to blend together and not much had changed.

One cold morning, grabbing my bag and pile of listing documents, I headed to the front door for another fun day of real estate uncertainty when Enemi said, "Your father has an eye doctor appointment today."

"So?" I grumbled, wondering why this would concern me. Dad's medical visits were usually routine, ending with the proclamation, "He's in perfect health."

"He wants you to go with us."

Stopping dead in my tracks, I sighed, annoyed. While Dad's medical appointments weren't on a daily basis like Mom's had been, he had a regular monthly visit to the eye doctor for the past two years, but my presence had never been required.

"But I've never been there before. Why now?"

"I think he just feels more comfortable with you there."

Patting my shoulder as she opened the door, Enemi giggled. "Who knows why old people do what they do, or why they want what they want." Then, with a look of all seriousness, she added, "You know his eyes are getting worse. He just may want a little extra support."

Walking to the car, I thought about my already exhausting schedule that day. With a new buyer wanting me to explore every home within a twenty-five-mile radius, I wasn't sure I could break away. After all, doctor visits on a good day took at least a couple of hours.

But, remembering the chat we'd had until 2:00 a.m. the night before about what it was like when he was little during the Great Depression, the war that followed, that I came to be named after him (my mom's sweet idea), and how he'd say at the end of every conversation, "I love you," I pulled out my phone, made some calls, and rescheduled my entire day.

I found myself hoping someone was watching upstairs. Maybe all this would make my way to heaven a little easier.

Three hours later, I met Enemi and Dad at the ophthalmologist. Walking into the waiting room, I saw my father sitting in his wheelchair in a corner and Enemi tapping away on her phone.

"Hi, Dad, I'm here," I said, kissing his cheek.

"Hi, honey. I'm so glad you came. I hate these visits," he mumbled, absently rubbing his forehead, head bowed as if in deep prayer.

I wondered how bad it could be to have a doctor look in your eyes. "What do they do to you?"

"They're trying to save my eyesight, so they put some medicine into my eye."

What's so tough about that? I wondered, feeling a little irritated at the inconvenience of being there.

"Do they just put some drops in?"

He stared at me blankly, and I wondered if he'd even heard me.

"Dad, do they just give you eye drops?"

He scratched his chin and looked around the room at the other poor souls waiting for their turn. "No, he has to stick a needle into my eye to get the medicine all the way to the back," he said reluctantly.

Bingo! No wonder he wanted me there.

"Ugh! That sounds awful. How many of these have you had?"

"One a month for I don't know how long."

Guilt washed over me as I found myself thinking, How did I not know this? I thought I knew everything about my parents and their ailments. How could I become so remiss as to not understand how horrible these visits were for him?

"Dad, I'm so sorry. I had no idea."

He patted my hand, his signal to say it was okay and that he was glad I was there.

An hour passed. Sitting confined in his prison on wheels caused his broken body a lot of pain.

"How much longer?" he moaned. "My back is aching."

Seeing the sweat on his neck soaking his collar, I looked over at Enemi, lost in her phone playing some stupid game called Candy Crush.

"Let me go find out."

As I walked past the other elderly patients, heads also bowed, I wondered if they too were beginning to live in the dark.

"Excuse me! Excuse me!" I called, patting the countertop of the nurse's station. "Hello! Is anyone there?"

As I waited impatiently, I found myself wondering what it must be like to be my dad. In her final years, my mother constantly lamented over the loss of her bodily functions, but he rarely said a word.

After she passed away, I'd often wondered what would be worse: to live with no legs and a sharp memory like my father, or a body with mobility but a brain floating on a cruise ship somewhere in the Pacific Ocean for an extended vacation around the world, but not knowing where in the hell it was. With my own body beginning its descent down the rabbit hole of ailments, nothing sounded good to me. Getting older was all just one big shit show.

Maybe medical science is letting us live longer than we should, I thought as I looked at all the ninety-plus-year-olds sitting with their caregivers. The Hippocratic oath prioritized preserving life at all costs, not only when the patient lived in their own personal hell, but when the family did as well. I swear if I get like this, I'm going to tell the kids to get my wheelchair to the Golden Gate Bridge and turn around. I'll take care of the rest. This is no way to live.

All of a sudden, I heard, "Can I help you?"

From behind the counter, a perky little nurse with Betty Boop lips appeared.

"Jack Madden has been waiting over an hour. How much longer?"

Looking over the roster, her gleaming Pepsodent smile lit up. "Only four ahead of him."

Suddenly, I felt my body want to lunge over the wall between us, grab her throat, and shake her silly.

"Four! That means at least another half hour." My voice rose, trembling in anger.

"I'm sorry for the inconvenience." Her plastic grin dimmed. "It won't be much longer."

"Me too," I hissed. "It's not like I don't have anything better to do. You know, a lot of us have jobs to get back to."

Marching back to my father, I sat down and held his hand. "Not too much longer. Can you close your eyes and take a rest?" Knowing Dad could sleep anywhere at a moment's given notice, my suggestion immediately sent him into a peaceful snore. Forty-five minutes later, we were called in.

"Hi, Mr. Madden," an annoyingly happy nurse with Little Orphan Annie curls and a turned-up nose sang. "Good to see you again."

Interrupting her happy reunion, I demanded, "How long do these things take?"

Shocked at my rudeness, she picked up dad's file, and in a high-pitched, pissy tone announced, "When the doctor is finished."

Great. Made a new friend today.

Five minutes later, another nurse waddled in.

"Mr. Madden, we need to get these drops in your eyes. I know they sting, but they will open up the pupil so the doctor can give you the shot."

Having heard it all before, Dad replied, "Yeah, yeah."

Tilting his head back, down went the liquid, drop by drop, into his good eye. The other one was too far gone.

"Okay, we'll let that sit for a few minutes. Now let's get you into the exam chair."

After she pressed the button on the wall to call for help, two buff male attendants with rolled-up sleeves exposing arms of steel arrived to lift Dad out of the wheelchair and onto the examining lounge.

"The doctor will come in shortly."

As she went merrily on her way, I thought about all the times he had to endure this nonsense. I also found myself burning with remorse that I was never with him. God knows I didn't miss any of Mom's appointments. Why had I become so lax with his care?

Maybe it was partly because I knew Enemi could handle it. I was a busy woman after all. But perhaps it was because I was sick of the whole goddamn caregiving thing. From the time I was twenty years old, Mom's health had begun to deteriorate with her first mastectomy, and so began my daughterly duties.

The year was 1972 and I was beginning intersession at the University of San Francisco—a six-week period between fall and spring semester where students were encouraged to take a class. I always felt making money was a better plan, so I worked every January at the upper crust department store, I. Magnin's, selling designer clothing to rich, snotty women.

When the chance of my mother needing a mastectomy became a reality, I left the possibility of a paycheck and went home to care for her instead. Dad helped in the way he could, but he fainted at the sight of blood. It was a routine I'd find myself in for the next thirty years, leaving my life to help my mom as one ailment after another spread all over her body. It wasn't long before much of our time together was either spent in a hospital or a doctor's office.

Remorse was now pouring over my self-perceived neglect

of Dad's care like warm maple syrup on our Sunday pancakes. Before I knew it, I was drowning in it.

"Jackie," Dad called, waking me from my bad girl moment. "I think this is going to help. Thank you for bringing me."

I patted his arm. "No problem. I'm happy to be here."

For the next twenty minutes, we again sat in silence: he obviously in prayer, me wallowing in all the ways I'd abandoned him in the past. Just then, a man-child entered the room.

"Hi, Jack," his doctor said, as if he were an old drinking buddy ponying up to the bar. Obviously, they were now on a first name basis since these monthly appointments had gone on for so long. "Let's take a look."

With his magnifying glasses, Dr. Thirty-something peered deep into the black cavern just beyond my father's blue eyes.

"All right, get ready. Here we go."

Taking a syringe the length of a ruler, he pierced the center of the eyeball, shot in whatever the hell he was shooting, then slowly drew it out.

"Okay, that should do it for now. I'll see you in a month."

See you in a month? Wait a minute. How's he doing? Is this shit even working?

It was time Mr. Fresh-out-of-med-school and I had a little conversation.

"Doctor, can I talk to you in private?" I asked softly so Dad wouldn't hear.

Fortunately, because my father's hearing had also become impaired, we didn't need to leave the room to have our tête-à-tête.

"What are you doing and is it working?" I whispered, my voice becoming less affable.

"Your dad has macular degeneration."

"I know that, but what the hell is it?"

"He still has his periphery vision."

Annoyed to the point of wanting to rip my hair out, my voice sizzled as I said, "I still don't understand what he can see and if this is doing any good."

Working on maintaining his bedside manner, the young doctor drew a picture of the eyeball: a circle with the pupil and iris in the middle.

"Okay, this is the eye."

Then, taking a black marker out of his pocket, he covered the entire center of the diagram in black.

"In a nut shell, this is what your dad sees."

Horrified, my eyes misted over. I knew he couldn't see much. I had been told a million times. But visualizing what it was actually like to be him, the true fact that his world had gone black, I died inside. No wonder he closed them all the time. Life is so much better living in memory when you can't see today.

"With the medication, we're just trying to keep what he has left."

"So it's not going to get any better."

"No."

"And what can he see now?"

"His other eye is gone and there's virtually nothing left here either."

"Then why are we torturing him by coming every month just to sit in the waiting room for an hour and a half for a shot that will not give him back his sight?"

With his pinched face showing his annoyance, he stuck

his pen in his pocket and said with a huff, "He has another appointment next month." The young doctor left the room.

Furious, I wanted to kick over all the medical apparatuses in the room. My sweet dad had been led to believe all this shit would bring back his eyesight. These appointments were just lessons in futility and a waste of a lot of money.

Goddamn doctors! Yeah, let's treat the patient even if it does no good. You get paid and they get to live in an empty soda can of false belief.

"What did the doctor have to say?" Dad asked, interrupting my angry moment. "Am I getting better?"

Looking at this soul who only deserved the best in life, I felt rage burning through my entire body. I wanted to lie and tell him it was working and that we'd be back in a month. But this was a moment he deserved the truth so he could once again move on. Dad had a miraculous way of accepting bad news. He might shut down for a while, maybe even days, but when he surrendered the pain back to God, a trick he was always trying to teach me, he moved on.

Leaning in, nearly cheek-to-cheek so he could hear my words clearly, I relayed, "Dad, your eyes have gotten really bad. There's nothing more they can do."

"But I'm going to see again, right? I have all those books I need to read," he implored.

Studying his face filled with optimism, I wanted to die. He always believed in the best, that life would be kind and God would be fair.

"No, Dad. You're never going to be able to read again. I'm so sorry."

Dropping his chin to his chest, he went still. Then, too upset to speak, I saw him mouth the words, "It's time to go home. We're not going to do this again."

As we walked out of the clinic that day, the rage I felt toward the medical profession was greater than any anger I had experienced in my life. Even more than struggling by myself to keep four teenagers out of harm's way as a single mother, or the time my mother passed away in a cold hospital where the care she was given diminished to nothing more than a pulse reading every few hours.

But my true fury was with God. Where was He now? Dad prayed all the time for guidance and help. He said it worked, but I was afraid He was on some island in the South Pacific, taking a break from all the madness in the world, with no cell phone service. One thing was for sure—he wasn't listening to my cries.

Wheeling Dad to the car, I stopped for a moment, stood behind his chair like so many other times in the past, and wrapped my arms around his neck, holding him close.

"Dad, I love you so much," I began, swallowing the tears that would come later. "I know this isn't what you wanted to hear, but we'll find a way to make it better."

Then, kissing him one last time, I turned him over to Enemi and let her take it from there. It was time I went back to work.

Pulling out of the parking lot, I found myself dealing with a recurring habit since he moved in: I began to sob uncontrollably.

"This is just too much!" I screamed, slamming my fists on the steering wheel. "When will he get a break?"

Mopping up my water-soaked cheeks, I worried how I would make this right for him. I could buy books on tape. That would help to take care of the unread library he wanted to tackle. I could ply him with extra treats. I could spend more time with him during the day. I could, I could, I could . . . But nothing would make this truly okay.

As I sat on the side of the road trying to regain my composure, I realized the most important thing I could do for my father was never lie to him. While some information might be painful and not what he wanted to hear, he deserved the truth. After all, it was what he always gave me.

1955 - David, Dad, Tim, and Me.

1979 - Dancing with my favorite partner.

1977 - Dad and me sharing a special moment.

1979 - The first man who ever loved me.

2010 - Our last dance together.

1958 - David, Mom, Michael, Dad, Tim, and Me.

1948 - Jack and Lassie Madden begin their life together.

2004 - The story begins as a single mother. Me, Timmy, Jenny, Lauren, Michelle.

1952 - From the moment I was born, he was my soul mate.

1971 - Dad and his favorite girl.

CHAPTER 12

Untold Sins

Christmas came and went without a lot of fanfare and I eventually stopped seething once I saw that Dad had accepted the bad news about his eyes. He was beginning to love spending his days with his headset on while listening to the latest novel on the *New York Times* best seller's list.

"I see you're enjoying that story," I said as he took the headphones off to have a snack.

"Yes! What a life that Kennedy family lived, and so much tragedy," he said, grabbing a chocolate chip cookie. "This has to be one of my favorites so far."

This recent story was *After Camelot: A Personal History of the Kennedy Family—1968 to the Present*—a time in history Dad seemed connected to.

I had never seen my father look so happy about a presidency than when John Kennedy took office in 1961. The fact that an Irish Catholic had risen to that level, plus that they were the same age, brought him indescribable joy.

"You know, the Irish had it rough in this country for many years," he began. "We had to fight hard to be noticed as anything other than drunks and bums." Savoring every morsel, he chewed on his cookie before continuing, "There was a political cartoonist in the late 1800s that pictured us as barbarians. I think his name was Thomas Nast. He coined the phrase 'No Irish need apply.'"

As a little girl, while my father rarely had much to say, the one thing he did talk about was how proud he was to be both Irish and Catholic and that, in his humble opinion, those were parts of our heritage that we should be grateful for as well. Our roots were steeped in tradition and tenacity that helped a beaten-down part of the human race to rise above poverty and illiteracy.

"Why do you think it was so hard for them? It wasn't like they weren't white or didn't speak English."

Gobbling up the last bit of his treat, he began my history lesson of the day.

"I think it's because the Irish were so poor when they first arrived to escape the Potato Famine. Nobody had any skills other than working in the fields, and when we came, we came in droves to the urban areas, upsetting those who already lived here. Kind of like how people feel about the Chinese and Indians these days that have bought so much property in the Bay Area. Plus, the United States was mostly Protestant at the time."

"Yeah, I can see how that could have happened. People fear what they don't understand. I'm sure all the new Roman Catholics setting up shop must have really made the Protestants crazy, especially when they started building churches on every corner."

Nodding, he giggled. "Yes, we got them good."

Listening to him talk, I began to wonder if his religion was more a part of his identification with Irish culture than something he believed in, and that's why he followed it so rigidly. I always struggled with the regulations Rome dumped on her tribe. Yet he never questioned the rules and dutifully did as he was told: no meat on Friday, attend Mass every Sunday, give up dessert during Lent, and listen to the direction of the Pope.

"Was it hard for you? I know your parents felt the discrimination. Did you feel it too?"

"By the time I was born, things were beginning to get better. Dad had become a finish carpenter, creating the elaborate moldings, window casings, and banisters on many Victorian homes. With the money they saved, Mom bought a couple of flats. We always lived on the top floor and rented out the bottom."

Looking out the window, he fell quiet as the memories returned. "But I'm not sure my mom ever got over the prejudice."

As he continued to talk, I recollected hearing what a tough beginning she had. At the age of four, my great-grandfather passed away, leaving my great-grandmother nearly destitute and in poor health. To help the situation in Ireland, my grandmother's sister Mary (who was fifteen years older) sent my grandmother to live in San Francisco until things got better. Getting on a boat with her sixteen-year-old brother Patrick, the two of them sailed across the Atlantic in 1871, sleeping in steerage with the other poor souls with only the clothes on their backs and a dream for a better life.

Upon reaching New York, they were ushered through Ellis Island, where her name was changed from Johanna to Josephine. Next, they traveled across the country by train until they finally reached their destination.

"Why do you think Grandma never got over it? Wasn't life better for her here?"

"In some ways, yes—at least she had food. But because she was older than her nieces and nephews, my aunt often used her as the babysitter instead of treating her like a sister. She was never allowed to be a little girl."

Thinking back to the times I spent a part of my summer vacation with my grandmother in San Francisco, the one thing that always stuck with me was how negative she was toward other races. Blacks were not to be talked to; in fact, we crossed to the other side of the street whenever possible. Chinese were stupid and Hispanics were just dirty. Perhaps when you've spent much of your life being pushed down, it makes you feel better to push down someone else.

"What was Grandma like as a mother?" I asked, wondering if her difficult life caused her to be tough with her children.

"She was very loving," my father said wistfully, casting a look at the family photo on the table nearby of his mother with her three young children. "She was strong, and in our family, she ruled the house because Dad was very quiet, but I never doubted she or my father loved me."

That's the same way I've always felt about you and Mom, I thought, smiling. *You learned that lesson well, Dad.*

Our intimate late-night talks were now spreading to our daytime conversations too. He had memories to share and I was his captive audience.

As he was about to plug into his book again, I decided to ask him something that had been burning in me since the day he moved in. I thought I already knew the answer, being the staunch Catholic he was, but I just had to ask.

"Dad, are you afraid to die?"

What came next confounded the hell out of me. Without hesitation, deliberation, or annoyance, he blurted out, "I'm terrified."

Pulling my chair closer to him, I wondered what all this faith stuff was for if you were still scared at the end. Wasn't believing supposed to relieve some of the angst of leaving this earth? After all, you got to be with your maker and sit on some fluffy white cloud with all the people who went before.

"I'm surprised you'd say that. Your faith is so strong."

"Just because your faith is strong doesn't mean you get to go to heaven."

Watching his chin begin to drop on his chest, I knew I was about to lose him to that quiet place he retreated to when things became difficult.

"Dad, what are you talking about, not going to heaven?" I said, interrupting his evacuation process.

Rubbing his forehead vigorously, as if trying to wipe away his anxiety, he let out his fear.

"Well, we may not all be in heaven in the end."

"Not be in heaven together? Why would you say that?" I asked, starting to get upset and wanting to get to the bottom of this silly nonsense.

The room became quiet as he looked out the window, watching those silly little birds instead of finishing this important conversation.

"Dad, talk to me. Who's not going to heaven?"

"None of you kids go to church. You have to go to church to go to heaven."

Oh boy! Here we go. How could such a brilliant man believe all this bullshit?

"That's ridiculous! What about the other religions that don't have that mandatory requirement?" I countered.

As the redness in his face showed his rising distress, I knew I had to rein him in or lose him to sleep for the next several days.

"Dad, I'm not half the person you are and I know I'm going to heaven. You raised fine young men too. They'll be there with all of us."

Seeing I was getting nowhere as his eyes locked onto a sparrow pecking the ground, I took his chin and turned it in my direction. "Look, you gave us the gift of faith. But when you give a gift, you can't tell people how to use it. Your parents gave you the same gift, and you chose to follow as tradition taught. We have chosen a different way to honor it, but it doesn't mean we don't value it, or believe in a higher power."

As he cast his eyes downward, I went in for the kill.

"You raised four kind, loving, moral Christian children. We'll all be in heaven one day together. God and I have already talked about it."

"Not if you have a mortal sin."

"What?"

Mortal sin was the deadliest of all sins. Who the hell in our family had that? I knew it wasn't me. Sure, I had done a lot of questionable things in my life, but I was still a good girl. As for David and Tim, there were no two finer men walking this earth. The only thing I could imagine was that Dad knew something about the baby of the family that we didn't. Michael had always traveled a different path, which was often heartbreaking to handle, but even he wasn't that egregious to travel to the dark side. Or was he?

"Dad, who are you talking about?"

The minute that he sat silently felt like an hour. Finally, shaking his head, he did what he always did when not wanting to face something. He shut down.

"I don't want to talk about this anymore."

"Wait! Are you talking about you?"

I couldn't imagine what he could have done that was so bad. He'd lived by the Golden Rule since the day he was born, prayed all the time, and helped the priests with their taxes at no charge. Suddenly, I realized that this was a deep, sore subject. The kind that keeps you awake at night fearing someone might find out about the real you.

Leaning in, I suggested, "Would you like to see a priest?"

His silence became cavernous. Then he nodded his head. "Yes."

Walking into my bedroom, I immediately picked up the phone and made a call to my parish, St. Simon Church. We had several priests, all kind and thoughtful, but for something as severe as mortal sin, I needed to pull out the big guns: the CEO. I asked for the pastor, Father Warwick James.

"Hi Father," I began. "My ninety-five-year-old father lives with me, and he's troubled about something in his past. Would you have time to stop by and visit him?"

While we had never been properly introduced, Father Warwick's reputation proceeded him as a caring man to those confined. Originally from South Africa, he spoke perfect English with a British accent, a rarity in the Catholic Church as many of the priests came from third world countries. He was tall, balding at the top, and had large, round, knowing eyes.

"Yes, love. How about this Tuesday?" I heard on the other end of the line.

Relieved to know Dad would have some peace in his future, I set the appointment.

Two days later, Father Warwick arrived in everyday clothes, prayer book in hand, looking like one of Dad's church-going buddies coming to check in on him.

"Thank you so much, Father." I shook his hand.

"Have you been a member of the parish long? I don't think I've ever seen you in church."

Skirting the issue, I talked about my children, how they were all baptized, had received their First Holy Communions and Confirmations at St. Simon, and the wonderful education they had at the school.

"So you've been a member for a long time," he said, his eyebrows lifting as if to ask, "Where the hell have you been all these years?"

"Yes, thirty-one years to be exact," I said, smiling but then I told a little white lie. "I'm out of town a lot and find other churches to go to when I'm not home."

Walking through the house, we found Dad in the family room waiting for his purification.

"Dad, this is Father Warwick."

Looking up, he smiled that contagious grin of his and stretched out his good hand.

"Hello, Father. Thank you for coming."

Pulling up a chair for Father Warwick next to him, they talked about generalities at first: Dad's upbringing and education (all Catholic, of course), where his four children were today, my mom, and when he'd most recently received communion.

Wanting them to get to the point of the visit, for I knew his worry was burning a hole in his immortal soul, I softly interrupted, "Dad, Father can give you confession if you'd like."

When he nodded his head in agreement, it was time for me to leave, for this was private stuff.

"Okay, I'll be down the hall in Lauren's room working," I said. "Call me when you're done."

Reaching Lauren's bedroom, I began to sense there was something wrong as the silence in the family room deepened. There were no voices, not even the hum of a whisper. Were they just staring at each other? Tiptoeing back, I wanted to be sure everything was okay, and that Dad hadn't lost his nerve. Then, I heard Father Warwick say, "Jack, there's nothing you can tell me that I haven't heard before."

My dad cleared his throat, and more silence followed. Then came the zinger.

"Well, Father, there was once this woman . . ."

Woman? What woman? Was it before you and Mom got married? Did you stray along the way? When did this happen and why didn't you ever confess it before?

Putting my fingers in my ears so as not to hear any more, I quickly went back to the bedroom and closed the door. Sitting down, my thoughts ran wild.

Some woman? It must have been before my parents got married. He said a lot of women were after him. But what if it wasn't? Was Dad unfaithful to Mom? Maybe he's not the man I thought he was. Maybe he's not so good after all. Maybe his persona all these years was just some great lie and he duped all of us into believing he was a saint.

Soon, my face began to burn and tears smarted my eyes. I

was in the process of mourning the loss of the man I thought he was.

I know we're innocent until proven guilty, but I heard it! Some woman caused my father to lose himself. Who was this slut taking advantage of such a gentle soul, and what a stooge he was for falling victim! Men can be so pitifully weak.

Staring at the photos on Lauren's desk, I wondered if my kids had secrets they needed to confess. Did I have secrets? Of course not. As a writer, I told the world everything. I would, of course, like to forget my biggie from a lifetime before.

In 1978, nine months before I married Dave, I found myself in the darkest of times and deepest of sins: I was pregnant. And I knew good girls didn't get pregnant before getting married. It was out of order and would be a complete disgrace.

Fearful of what this news would do to my mother, whose health had already started its downward spiral and who was constantly worried about the direction that my youngest brother Michael was taking with his life, I just couldn't bring shame to the family name. Despite the fact that it was Dave's child and we'd be married the following year, we made a decision that would haunt me for many years to come.

On a bitterly cold December morning, I made the trip to Planned Parenthood with my child's father, and together we gave her away, back to God. Six years later I'd be seeking my priest for absolution.

Thinking of my own indiscretion, how could I ever judge my father? He knew about mine when he read about it in my first book, and he never said a thing. Only that he loved my story. Suddenly, I began to sob.

After a few minutes, a calm slowly came over me. Dad's

sin compared to mine was like a granite pebble next to the mountain it fell off of. But in the eyes of the Church and her rules, you didn't even need to touch the opposite sex. Just let those eyeballs wander with a little lust and boom, you're doomed to hell. Unless, of course, you found a nice priest who could give you five Hail Marys and make the sign of the cross over your head. Then you'd be washed clean again, ready for heaven whenever the dear Lord called.

As I pulled myself together, I got over his possible feet of clay, and I found myself loving my father more than I ever did before. He wasn't a saint and he wasn't perfect. He was like all of us, another one of God's children trying to make his way through the labyrinth of life and all her detours.

Hearing their conversation wrapping up, I wiped my eyes, fluffed my hair, and joined the two men.

"Thank you so much, Father," Dad said, his eyes now sparkling.

"I'll come back again if you'd like. I enjoyed our conversation."

"Yes, I'd like that."

Walking the priest to the door, I took his hand in both of mine, and thanked him profusely.

"This meant so much to him. Thank you."

"You have a remarkable man for a father. I hope you know that."

Looking into the deep pools of his eyes, my heart warm and grateful, I acknowledged what I had known all along. "Yes, I know. I'm truly blessed."

CHAPTER 13

Back to Church

After seeing Father Warwick out the door, I went back to the family room to check on my dad. He faintly smiled as he watched his winged friends outside. It was the same smile he gave when he was in awe of God's beauty in the world—serene and at complete peace.

"Do you feel better?" I asked, sitting in the chair the priest had just vacated.

"Oh, honey, thank you! Yes, I feel so much better."

"Good. Would you like to continue to listen to your book? I think you're at the part where David Kennedy loses his life to drug addiction."

With his blue eyes staring thoughtfully, I could tell he had something on his mind. Maybe he wanted to tell me about the woman, or maybe he had another story to share from his childhood. Whatever it was, I'd be a captive audience, as always, despite the fact that I should've been heading to the office.

"I'd like to talk to you about something," he began beseechingly.

"Sure, Dad. What is it?"

"I want you to go back to church."

As if I'd just been told to eat a big chunk of liver with no condiments, I grimaced. Why did he have to spoil this lovely moment with talk of church? Couldn't he see I was doing just fine without it?

Taking a deep breath, I prepared myself for battle.

"I don't need to go to church to feel close to God. Now let's put those headphones on."

"It would make me so happy."

"Would you like a cookie to go with your story? We still have some."

"When was the last time you went?" he needled.

"I think there's a baseball game on tonight. We'll have to be sure to watch it together."

"Jackie . . ."

Knowing there was no way to skirt this topic, for he seemed intent on converting someone who had already been converted at birth, I sighed. "I just can't go, Dad. You need twenty-four-hour care. I can't leave you alone."

He arched his eyebrows as we stared at each other.

"You can leave me alone for forty-five minutes. You don't have to stay until the end. Just receive communion and go."

I thought about his will, I held the power of attorney, which meant I was not only responsible for his finances, but his health directive as well. It was a job I took very seriously.

"Dad, I can't do that. What if something happened while I was gone, like an earthquake or fire? I'd be held accountable for what happened to you."

"That's not going to happen."

"You don't know that. An earthquake could happen at any time. And you already experienced one fire in your home."

Tilting his head, he tapped his chin with his index finger.

I could tell by the look in his eyes he was calculating his next move, as if I were a pawn on a chess board and he was the knight coming to knock me off the board completely. When it came to matters of religion, he was relentless.

"Dad! I'd be charged with elder abuse if anything happened."

The room became deathly quiet. He wanted what he wanted. He was old, and he should have it. I was stubborn and unkind not to grant him this simple wish.

Sure, if I really wanted to go, I could find a way. I could tell a neighbor I'd be out of the house for a little bit and that he was home alone. I could hire a young girl to act as a babysitter, only in this case, a daddy-sitter.

I sat there, feeling uncomfortable with the topic and afraid to tell him the real truth as to why I no longer found peace and meaning in Mass.

"If you must know the truth, going to church makes me sad."

Stunned, his eyes grew wide and mouth gaped open. I could see by his expression he was thinking, How could this be? Going to church brings me such peace and joy. What did I do wrong?

"Dad, it has nothing to do with me not believing. My entire life I've wanted to live a Christ-like existence, so please, don't go thinking you and Mom did anything wrong or that the nuns screwed up."

Shifting in my seat, I suddenly remembered the day at the eye doctor when I decided he always deserved the truth. While he may pooh-pooh my reasoning, it was my truth all the same.

"To be perfectly honest, I don't fit there anymore."

He took a deep breath. He knew it was best not to argue

but to console. "That's silly, honey. The one place you always belong is in church."

Tears fogging my eyes, I wondered how I could tell someone as devout as him that I felt that God had abandoned me. It was one thing to be rejected by my husband. That cliché happens all the time: boy meets girl, boy marries girl, together they have a beautiful family, and one day, girl no longer serves the purpose. Boy dumps girl. I was part of the 50/50 club—50% stay married, 50% get divorced. But God was supposed to help me pick up the pieces. I wasn't supposed to feel this lonely or lost.

"Dad, I don't want this to sound like a pity party. Well, maybe it is, but when Dave left, my life was a mess. Mom was dying, the kids were all teenagers and angry with him but taking it out on me, and I was scared of how I'd keep everything together financially. God was nowhere around to ease the pain."

Dad was giving me an "are you serious?" look, and I could hear how stupid this all sounded. Sure, it was a crappy time in my life, but I had survived. I suppose I couldn't have done that if God hadn't been waiting in the wings.

The mist in my eyes began to turn into droplets. It seemed that since my father moved in with me, all I did was cry.

"Jackie," he said, his tone now soft and empathic. "Church is the one place everyone should go to release their fears and sorrow."

"Not when I'm surrounded by couples with their kids. I'm all alone."

There, I said it—the real reason I didn't want to go to church. When I got divorced, my social world changed too. I was no longer a couple and, in my tired mind, couples only did things with other couples.

Digesting my every word, Dad reached out for my hand. "Honey, I understand. You were once part of a huge social circle, and now you feel all alone."

With his validation of my feelings, I let the rest sputter out.

"Dave and I always organized so many of the fun events, and not just for couples but the kids too. We opened our home up every weekend in the summer for potlucks and planned vacations where everyone came. Now, I'm never invited to those kinds of things. Unless it's a group affair, like a wedding or celebration, I feel like I don't exist."

"Do you think you'd be comfortable going out to dinner or on a trip if you were the only single woman?"

"I don't know, maybe. It's not like the couples sit together. Women typically talk to each other while the men hang around at the bar. What harm would it be to have a stray along?"

Compassion washing over his face, my father said, "Honey, while I know this has all been hard for you, I have a feeling this is all stuff you've created in your mind. I know your friends love you. People just get busy with their lives and time goes by. Before you know it, a week becomes a year. It happens to everyone."

Thinking about his words, I saw that once again, any emotions I had about the stations in my life were ones I created. No one ever did anything to me but be kind but, just the same, I hurt and I wanted to wallow in the pain.

"It's just better not to relive the past, and that includes going to church," I said.

Getting up to leave, I pulled my hair back from my face and leaned in and kissed him.

"Honey, I promise if you go back with an open mind you'll find some happiness there. It's where I've turned in my darkest hours."

Seeing how important this was to him, and how I was determined to make his life perfect, I grabbed his headphones, got the CD player ready for the next chapter, and promised, "Okay, I'll try."

For the next several days, I stewed over the idea. I was already in so much pain as it was. Did I really want to pour gasoline on the campfire? I could just lie and say I went. Or I could go to church but sit in the parking lot. That wasn't lying. I was there. I could just as easily pray in my car as I could in the building. But, remembering a promise was a promise, I called my neighbor's daughter, Kelly, and asked if she'd sit with Dad for an hour. I'd be paying her to do nothing.

That Sunday evening, much to Dad's delight, I left for 5:00 p.m. Mass, ready to deal with the past. Arriving five minutes early, I found an empty pew at the back of the church.

This was perfect. If I couldn't stand it, I could just slip out, and no one would see me.

Soon, the choir began to sing, and a visiting priest paraded down the aisle with two young altar servers dressed in white like angels. Remembering Jenni in that same outfit, I smiled. Watching her serious face while taking on her duties on the altar always made me giggle. Like her mother, she was the über good girl who wanted to be close to God as a child.

After the music had ended, the priest began to talk in what might have been English but sounded more like tongues. I couldn't understand a thing he was saying.

I come for peace, and now all I am is frustrated. I have no idea what the hell he's saying with that accent. He could be telling a dirty joke, and we'd never know.

With my concentration fading, I knew I had about a half hour left and began to spend it doing more productive things. Macy's was having a huge sale, and I calculated my finances to determine if I had enough to go on a shopping spree. Next, I made mental notes of the week to come, the appointments that were to be kept, and the Lifetime movie on Wednesday I didn't want to forget.

Suddenly, we were all standing, holding hands and saying the Our Father.

Just a few more minutes and I'd be out of there.

Communion quickly followed. Like in all the years past, I walked up with the crowd, stretched out my hands and received the body of Christ. Making the sign of the cross, I struggled to swallow the sticky thin wafer as it stuck to the roof of my mouth and headed to the back of the church, past the holy water, out the door, and straight for my car, thinking about the glass of wine I'd pour myself as soon as I got home.

"Thanks, Kelly," I said, paying her ten bucks for doing her homework. "Did he want anything?'

"No, he just slept."

"What else is new?"

"If you ever need more help, just let me know. I bet you'd like to get out once in a while."

Looking at the eighteen-year-old college student, I smiled. "You are so wise. I'll do that."

Well, maybe the one good thing out of all this is knowing I have a little freedom once in a while if I want.

Going into his bedroom, I watched the snoring gentle giant.

I'd kept my promise. I went, and I didn't just sit in the car. I was a good girl.

Seeing his sheet had fallen to the side, I carefully lifted it up and over to cover him. Sensing my presence, his eyes shot open.

"Well, what did you think?"

"I went. It was okay, but I couldn't understand a thing the priest said."

"That doesn't matter. Take it as your time alone with Christ."

Then, grabbing his beads, for it was now time for his Mass, he asked, "Are you going again next week?"

Are you kidding me? I did it once. Isn't that good enough?

"It would make me very happy."

Turning the TV on, I patted his shoulder and said, "Okay, for you, I'll do it."

"I want you to do it for yourself, but if it starts with doing it for me, then I'm good with that."

As he wiggled his head deeper into the pillow to get comfortable, I left to get that glass of wine.

Dad, for you I'd do anything, but this one is tough.

For the following weeks, the routine was always the same. One of the three daddy sitters I discovered (Kelly Cheek, Cassie O'Hearn, and Elizabeth Cook), came so I could sit in the back and think about more important things like laundry, groceries, and clearing land mines the dog left on the lawn so the gardener could mow poop free. I grabbed the wafer, pretended it meant something, and immediately ran home for my wine. And each time Dad smiled.

"That's good," he said with his dimpled chin grin. "You made me happy."

Five Sundays later, the idea of going to a bar instead began to tickle my fancy. They gave you wine in church. Dad would never know I went someplace else to get it. But that evening, something changed.

Sitting once again with the exit sign screaming my name, I was surprised to see Father Warwick was the presider. He'd been to the house several more times to chat with Dad, and I marveled at his patience over some of Dad's questions. Dad was still working through his issues with leaving this world.

"Father, what do we look like when we die?" he had asked at the most recent visit. Most of his questions centered on dogma, but this was weird.

"Well, Jack, I'm not sure, but I don't believe we will look like this."

"So, we won't have our bodies?"

"Most likely not. We will be in spirit form. Why do you ask?"

"Well, I've been thinking. There've been millions of people since time began. I was just wondering, where does God put them all? It could get crowded up there."

Hearing this, I laughed uncontrollably. My father always hated crowds. Was that what was keeping him from wanting to go? Every time we talked about the end, I'd hear a resounding "I'm not ready."

Sitting in the pew, I felt it only polite that maybe this time, I would try to listen and be a little more present. After all, since he'd been so good to Dad, I owed him that much.

Listening to his thoughts about humanity and our blessings, I began to look around the church with new eyes. People of all ages—some married, some not, some with their children and some alone—were there to celebrate in kinship and embrace our higher power. Lovely memories washed over me as I watched children huddle close to their parents just as mine had so long ago, finding a way to snuggle in my lap as I lowered my head in prayer. Maybe I was wrong. Maybe church was the one place I did belong. I just had to let go of my ego and let my spiritual side celebrate.

Going home that night, I went straight to my father before releasing Kelly.

"How was it?" he asked hopefully.

"Dad, it was great. I'm glad I went. And, guess what? You'll be happy to know I plan to continue going. It brought a lot of peace to my heart."

"What about still feeling like you don't fit in with your friends?" he asked, concerned I was still lost.

"Dad, I know my friends love me. I guess I just get lonely sometimes and want to blame the world for what I feel is lacking in my life."

He smiled, closed his eyes, and with an appreciative nod of the head, said, "That's good. You did just fine."

CHAPTER 14

All in a Day's Excitement

I once read that "Emotional stability leads to cognitive consistency. Cognitive consistency leads to behavioral predictability." This is all well and good when it comes to wanting to know how people react in any given situation, but when predictability shows, like how our days unfolded everyday with the same damn routine, this just lead to boredom.

A pattern had developed over the past nine months. We were well into 2012 and each day began and ended the same— no deviation, no thrills, no ups or downs. Other than the temperature rising and falling, plus an occasional breeze to shake things up, our home life was quiet, and I was becoming antsy for a change.

"Maybe everyone was right, Michelle," I said to my daughter on our daily phone call between Los Altos and Los Angeles. "I may not be cut out for this."

"Why, Mom? With Enemi there you can still get out during the day. It's not like you're in prison."

She had a point. By holding on to Enemi, I had some freedom to come and go between her new shortened hours of 9:00 a.m. to 3:00 p.m. But at night, when the house was still and the only sound that could be heard was Dad's raspy snoring, prison sounded like a hell of a lot more fun. At least there the inmates created some excitement with an occasional riot or feeble breakout attempt.

"You're right. I need to always remind myself this could be far worse, but I wasn't prepared for the responsibility, nor the boredom. We talk about death a lot. At least I do."

"That's awful. Why are you talking about death? He's not going yet, is he?"

I thought back to the time just before he moved in when I talked with a psychic about whether I should take Dad in or not. What she saw in her crystal ball and tarot cards felt doable: he'd be gone in three months. In a few days, we would be at four times that. Fearful it could now happen at any time, I wanted all the bases covered.

"No, he's still healthy. It just makes me think about how I would have done things differently with your grandmother if I knew then what I know now," I explained.

My mother died in a cold, sterile hospital with bright lights that never dimmed, even in the dead of night, and an IV protruding from her veiny arm dripping massive amounts of morphine to act as comfort care. Because of all the narcotics she had been prescribed in her earlier years to reduce the pain in her body, she was an unintentional addict. To give her any more would have been considered an illegal dose. Her time in the hospital was torture for all of us, especially her, and I was not about to let this happen to Dad too.

"Like what? How or what could you have done differently? They only gave Grandma twenty-four hours to live. Who knew she'd last a week?" My child attempted to ease my guilt.

"I'd have taken her home to die. I'd have planned the funeral differently and made sure all her friends could be there, even if I had to pick them up myself. I'd have never left her side, not even for a second."

Hearing a pause on the other end of the line, I waited for my child's wisdom.

"Mom, you didn't know there were options, so stop feeling bad. Besides, it's not yours or anyone's responsibility to make death perfect. That's a journey we all have to take alone."

"But I need to know if he wants to die alone or with us with him. Does he want to be cremated? What music to play—"

"Oh, for God's sake, Mom." Michelle sighed, exasperated. "Look, Grandpa will die the way he sees fit. All you can do is love him."

Words to remember, but challenging in practice. After all, I was a mom and moms fix everything for everyone, including their aging fathers.

Coming home for my lunch break a few days later, I found him in his usual position with drool seeping from his cracked lips onto a paper napkin strategically placed on his shoulder. Deep into his zone, I noticed how limp and still he sat.

Is he sleeping or in a meditative trance? I wondered. I'd heard you can have an out-of-body experience if you go deep enough. That's one way to escape all this.

Tiptoeing to his side, fearful of startling him, I sat on the edge of the coffee table next to him. Studying the man who gave me half my chromosomes, the man I was named after, I thought about how little I knew about his life and all that was left to uncover. His introverted world was typically locked tight and I needed the right key to open up a conversation. In other words, he needed to be awake and in a talkative mood.

Tapping his arm, I whispered, "Dad, I'm home."

As if shocked by a defibrillator, he instantly opened his eyes. "Hi honey! I missed you. Got any new listings?"

Giggling, I smiled.

"No, Dad. Not today. Maybe tomorrow," I replied, patting his arm. "Maybe tomorrow."

For some strange reason, my father had the notion that getting a client to buy or sell a house was as easy as picking up the daily newspaper off the driveway.

"Yes, tomorrow." He nodded. "Always know, you're going to be just fine."

"How did you sleep last night?" I asked, moving my fingers through his thick mane. His hair needed cutting.

Rubbing his forehead with his good hand, he squinted. "Just awful. I was awake all night."

"You were? I checked you about 11:00 p.m. and you were sawing logs. In fact, you were snoring so loudly it sounded like you were taking down an entire forest."

"No, I was awake until the sun came up."

"But . . ."

"No, I'm telling you. I was awake all night."

Not wanting to argue, for my time was limited and I knew I'd lose the battle anyway, I let it go and changed direction.

"Would you like to read the mail?"

"Oh, yes, please."

Walking to the front door, I noticed a pile of unfolded laundry sitting on a chair. It was the same load that had been there when I left. In fact, it had been there since yesterday.

Annoyed, I wondered why it took Enemi so long to get the simplest of chores accomplished. She used to be on top of things. It wasn't like Dad kept her running in circles. From the moment she placed him in his chair until he was back in bed, she had five hours to herself.

What does she do all day? Maybe I should do this myself. I'm already cleaning the house, cooking, and doing all the grocery shopping. All she has to do is fold his clothes and put them away. Where in the hell is she?

But knowing I could never lift my father's body by myself, I knew I was trapped. I still needed help.

As I approached the front door, I noticed a brown mound curled up on the lounge chair in the living room. Rolled up as if she were about to do a cannon ball into the pool, Enemi had her fingers glued to her connection to the rest of the world, her cell phone, punching away on another game.

Ah, yes. That's what she does all day.

Enemi didn't like to read or watch TV. Not only did her phone keep her linked to her extended family with constant texts, but she also loved to play any game she could download for free. It was her source of entertainment.

"Hi," I called out, making my presence known.

She startled, looking up.

"Is everything okay?" she asked, quickly tucking her phone to her side.

"Everything's fine," I pretended, wanting her to look more alive than my father. "But there seems to be a ton of laundry. It's all Dad's stuff. Do you mind taking it into his room and folding it?"

As if a spring had burst through the cushion and bit her in her rear end, Enemi flew out of the chair.

"Sure, sure. I was just taking a break."

"Thanks. I'll be reading Dad his mail for the next half hour."

Reaching the mailbox, I found it overflowing like Christmas card heaven. Between two people getting the same amount of junk mail (at least five envelopes a piece), there were also newspaper advertisements, an occasional card, and your typical bills: PG&E, water, credit cards, mortgage, and phone.

Oh, look, David sent him a card, I thought, pleased, placing it on top of the pile. Carrying the stack inside, I prepared myself for his interrogation.

"What do I have today?" He smiled as if he were a five-year-old waiting for a party invitation.

"Looks like a lot of junk, people asking for money, and a couple of bills."

"Open them, please."

"Can I just read you your note and the bills? The rest is worthless."

Stirring in his chair, attempting to position himself upright, he widened his eyes and his face turned bright pink. I recognized the signs. He was anxious.

"No, please read them all. You just never know. There might be something very important."

Holding back my frustration—I had better things to do than read him mail that belonged in the bin—I sorted the pile in order of importance: David's letter, bank statements, bills, and junk.

"Your son David sent you a letter," I began, slitting it open. His face lit up.

"Dear Dad, I'm sending you this note to tell you I'm thinking of you. We're all doing fine and send our love," I read.

He smiled, but then looked away. As my father grew older,

his emotions were just under the surface, causing tears to spring to his eyes over the simplest things. The only time I saw him tear up in my youth was when I was in seventh grade and his mom suddenly passed away. Now it was almost a daily occurrence and always over a sweet gesture.

"He's such a good boy," he said softly, as he stared out the window. "A sweet, kind soul."

Realizing this might be a great opportunity to revisit the past, I answered, "Yes, Dad. He certainly is; he always has been. I think he was such a perfect little kid. How about the other boys?"

"Tim always amazes me," he continued, taking the napkin from his chin to wipe away a tear escaping down his cheek. "He was such a good little boy, too, you know."

That isn't the way I remember it, I wanted to say.

Tim and I were twenty months apart in age, and as children we looked like twins. But while I was an exemplary little girl, following every rule my parents put forth, Tim was a rascal, constantly getting himself into mischief and doing the opposite of what he was told. If my memory served me correctly, and it always did, my parents were constantly scolding him about something, whether it was falling out of a tree and breaking an arm or two, or his grades slipping. But I decided not to argue with my father's memory.

"And Michael?"

Tilting his head to look at the ceiling, he sat very still for a moment. I wondered what his response would be. Michael was the baby of the family and had been a beautiful one at that. With cobalt blue eyes, snow-white curls, and a dimple in his cheek that resembled Dad's, he was precious as a little boy, though less so much later in life.

"Michael was always quiet, but such a good boy."

As a surprise in their forties, after Mom's reproductive cycle had slowed down, our entire family rallied around this gift that arrived late in life—helping him with schoolwork, including him in our budding social lives, and protecting him long into his adult years, even when his choices became questionable in the eyes of social acceptability and the law.

I was happy to hear my father had only good memories, and not the ones that caused pain, anger, and screaming.

Finishing the list of my testosterone-loaded siblings, I was sure the best was being saved for last. After all, I was the only girl—his rose among the thorns. I was not only sweet but perfect. My mother always said so.

"How about me?" I asked, waiting to hear about my accolades.

"You? Oh, you were very busy."

Busy? What the hell did that mean?

"And sneaky."

Sneaky! Wait a minute! What about kind, loving, and giving?

For a moment, I felt a pang of resentment. Yes, it was true that I snuck quarters from his dresser drawer to buy a candy bar or two, but come on! I was the child who took care of all life's little messes, including his adult diapers. How come I wasn't good?

"Yeah, I had to keep my eye on you."

Shit, all David has to do is send a lousy one-dollar card, and he walks on water. I've given up my life, and all I get is sneaky!

But remembering he was old and needed to live with loving memories of his sons, I decided to move on, despite the sting to my ego.

Next, I opened the invoices and we discussed the payments due. I was just about to scoop up the rest and whisk them away to the trash when my dad stopped me.

"Those too. I want to read all of them."

"But Dad, it's just junk mail, I promise. Nothing important."

"I want to know what's in them. Please don't argue with me. My mail is important," he exclaimed.

I listened to his beseeching tone and carefully said again, "They're just charities asking for donations."

"I want to be sure."

Plopping myself back down, I opened the envelopes: Santa Clara County Catholic Charities, Children's Christian Fund, his alma maters St. Mary's College and Sacred Heart High School, and finally, the parish I grew up in, St. Charles Church. They all wanted money.

Jesus, all these Catholics ever do is ask for donations. Maybe they need to pray a little harder for manna from heaven and leave our wallets alone.

"Like I said, Dad. They all want money."

"Okay, throw them away." Patting my knee to show his appreciation, he turned away and announced, "I'm going to take a nap now."

I decided that next time, I would throw them away before he knew they were even in the pile.

Looking at the time, I still had fifteen minutes before I had to go back to work. Releasing Enemi for a stroll around the neighborhood, I went to sit in my bedroom to collect myself. Like the tread on a tire about to pop, I was worn out. Boredom had become my new normal. The life I once lived with friends and an occasional date had vanished. I'd been seeing a lovely

Englishman named Oliver for nearly two years, and while we were more friends than a couple, he too disappeared the moment my father moved in.

I could now see why Dad was so afraid of becoming a burden. I never realized what a burden boredom can be. Thank God he didn't move in sooner. I'd be in the looney bin by now.

Peering into the backyard, I saw our bird friends dancing merrily on the wind. How I wish I could be one of them right now, even for just a few minutes, and fly to somewhere new. Just as I was about to burst into full-blown tears, it hit me why reading his mail was so crucial.

Now ninety-six, Dad had outlived his entire family, my mother, and all his friends. The process of opening his mail made him feel linked to the world at large. Every time it arrived, it was a signal, a calling card, that he was still alive and that someone was thinking of him, even if they wanted money.

One day, I too may be just like him and would want to know my life still mattered, even if it came as an advertisement from AARP.

Going to the mirror, I dabbed at the black panda-like circles forming around my eyes.

"You were so sure you could handle this," I said to myself as I stared at my reflection. "You're such a fraud. You never believed he'd live this long—that's why you thought you could actually do it."

Pulling myself back together by reapplying my mascara and lipstick, I gathered my things and headed to the door as Enemi was coming back in.

"You off to work again?" she asked, wiping the sweat off her forehead with the edge of her blue and yellow sarong.

"Yeah, I need to go. I'll be back by 3:00 p.m."

Seeing the tired look in my eyes, she reached out and softly touched my arm.

"Jackie, I hope you know how much he loves you. He tells me all the time."

"He does?"

"Yes, he's always telling me what a sweet, wonderful girl you are and how lucky he is to have you as a daughter."

Despite his earlier remark about me being sneaky, I had to stop for a minute. While Dad sometimes had a hard time admitting he was wrong or discussing the depths of his emotions for another person to their face, the one thing I never doubted about either of my parents was that they loved their kids. They constantly showed it by the way they were selflessly there for each of us their entire lives.

"Thank you. I know. This has just turned out to be harder than I thought. But I'll get through it. Thank you for your help."

"I've taken care of a lot of old people in my life," she continued, moving closer for a hug. "Many are difficult. Your dad isn't always easy, but he's a good, kind man."

"Funny you should say that," I responded, hugging her back. "That's exactly how Mom always described him when we asked why she married him."

Walking to the car, I began to smile. Despite the fact he could be crabby, demanding, and annoying, I had to agree.

"He's a good man and he's worth all the inconvenience," I admitted out loud.

CHAPTER 15

Where Has All the Money Gone?

I slowly opened my eyes and stared at the ceiling. A tiny spider was working its way across the expanse of white paint, step by step, with slow determination. She was obviously on a mission to get somewhere, but where? Like a nomad crossing a vast desert of sand, with no food, water, or another living creature for thousands of miles, she trekked on her mission for survival. Studying her every step, I found myself envious. Like her, I was wandering alone across my own desert, but while she was able to hang on while walking upside down, it seemed every step I took sent me tumbling to the ground.

Regardless of the fact that we were entering springtime, the March temperatures continued to be bitterly cold. Each day, the wind whipped at my back, forcing me to layer up with sweaters, scarves, and coats. Winter was not giving up without a fight, very much like my father.

I can't believe Dad is still holding on, I thought, watching the wind torment the new buds opening on the maple tree outside my bedroom. Dad was sleeping more than ever now and our deep conversations had become rare.

"Are you okay?" my dear friend Sheri asked one evening

when I hired Cassie to watch Dad so I could go out to dinner. "I know you too well, and I can tell something's going on in that mind of yours."

Taking a gulp of wine, I didn't want to moan about the fact that my last commission check had been in November. Four months later, the money tree had yet to bloom with the ensuing spring.

"I'm okay." I tried to convince myself as much as her. "It just gets a little scary when the bills come in, and the funds are shrinking. But you know that all too well. It goes with being a realtor."

With an empathetic gaze, Sheri reached across the table and took my hand. "Do you want to borrow some? I'm happy to give it to you."

A tear found its way down my cheek, and I grabbed a napkin before it became a flood. Filled with gratitude, I answered, "I know you would. But I have to figure this out on my own. I guess I never took into account how expensive taking care of him would be."

"Doesn't your dad have any money?"

"That's my problem. He's sitting on over two million but refuses to spend it because he wants to leave his kids an inheritance."

Studying the pained look in my eyes, Sheri held my hand even tighter.

"I think you should start charging your dad's estate. I've heard that losing their income is one of the toughest things for caregivers."

"I can't do that. He's so proud of the money he's been able to save."

"Jackie, what would you be doing if you put him in a home? Would you be paying for that?"

Downing another swallow, I played with the soggy napkin. Of course I wouldn't pay if we had to put him in a facility. His life savings would go to that. But it would also kill him to know that everything he scrimped and saved was being eaten away, leaving nothing for his four kids. Parents of that generation wanted to leave behind a legacy, and that meant a wad of cash.

"Look, you have given your father such a gift by taking him in, but that doesn't mean your whole life has to stop."

"I know, but I volunteered to do this. And my whole life hasn't stopped. Now that I've got girls that will sit with Dad, I can get out once in a while in the evenings."

As the waitress brought our food, I felt a sigh of relief to get off the subject. Talking about it made it that much more real.

"And who pays for the girls to sit?" she asked, knowing the answer. "You have enough stress on your plate just making sure he has everything he needs. Financial overload wasn't part of the bargain."

Listening to her words, I thought how nice it would be to collect even a little stipend from his savings. I was now down to my last $25,000 with no deal in sight.

While in some parts of the world that's a fortune, in my little corner of the globe in Silicon Valley it was near the poverty level, especially when I had two properties—my home in Los Altos and a cabin in the Tahoe Mountains—to keep up and pay taxes on. My monthly expenses were $9,000. If something didn't break soon, I'd be in big doo-doo.

"I know what you're saying, but my mother raised me to be

completely self-sufficient and independent from the moment I could tie my shoes. Never in my entire life did I go to my parents and ask for a handout. I'm not about to now."

"What happens if you completely run out? You need to protect yourself."

I thought of all the times I'd hit rock bottom financially: during my college years when I lived on cottage cheese and ketchup, post-college days when a new dress or coat was paid off on layaway because I never had the full amount at the time of purchase, and after my divorce as I tried to educate our four kids. I sighed. Somehow, I always found a way.

"I'm so appreciative that you're worried, but I'll figure it out."

Later that evening, after handing a twenty-dollar bill to Cassie for doing her homework for several hours as my father slept, I sat down to the stack of invoices sitting on my desk awaiting payment and began to blubber. This was the lowest I'd been financially in a long time.

When Dad moved in, he gave me $400 a month for his food and medical necessities. While that easily covered the basics, what wasn't factored in were all the other costs.

Old people are prone to get chilly, whether in the dead of winter or during the warm summer months. With the heater cranked up 24/7 and the washer and dryer spinning in perpetual motion, the PG&E and water bills rose an extra $300 a month.

He was also devouring books on tape at the tune of two a week. I tried to take them out of the library, but inevitably they'd be scratched or missing a disk. So, to ensure pure listening satisfaction, I bought them, and those puppies came with a high price tag.

Factor in a night out once a week with a daddy-sitter, and by the end of the month, I was shelling out at least $100 so I could have a break.

Adding up all the miscellaneous expenses, it only came to an extra $400 to $500 a month, but with no money coming in, fear created the sensation of pouring hydrogen peroxide on an open wound: it stung like hell.

Thinking about Sheri's suggestion, I wondered if it was time to do a little hinting about my current financial status. I would never come right out and ask for help, for that was not in my nature. But if he got wind that his only daughter was suffering, perhaps he'd volunteer to help out.

Going into his room to check on him, I saw that he was wide awake. Mustering my courage, I decided it was best to speak in generalities.

"Boy, Dad, things have gotten expensive," I announced, fluffing his pillow before kissing his cheek. "I can't believe the price of eggs and detergent."

Studying my face with military attention, I could see he wasn't just hearing me, but listening to me.

Great! I've got his attention. He'd never want his girl to suffer. After all, he calls me his "pet" and his "special girl." Play this right, and I bet he'll up the ante.

Nodding, he put his index finger under his chin and said, "Yep, that's how life goes."

"Did you know milk is up to $3.00 a gallon?"

"I wouldn't doubt it. Things go up; then they come down."

"Even gas is outrageous."

"Did Cassie leave? She's a sweet kid."

"Dad, did you hear me? Gas is up to $3.60 a gallon!"

"That's a shame, but I don't drive a car anymore."

"Yeah, but I do." *And so does Enemi when she drives you, and I'm shelling out extra cash for that too.*

Realizing it was better to discuss items close to home, like his sanitary needs, I continued, "Even your diapers, wipes, and all those lotions have gone up in price."

"That's too bad."

Shit! Is he completely obtuse?

Getting nowhere, I let out a groan and announced I was going to turn on his music.

"You know, Jackie," he began, "I always wanted to teach you how to live by a budget, but you were never interested."

"What?" I found myself blurting as embers in my stomach quickly ignited. "I've never had problems with managing the household expenses," I roared back argumentatively.

Looking at me, his face conveyed that same fatherly love I'd witnessed throughout my life when he felt proud of my accomplishments.

Oh goodie, he's going to throw me a bone. I can feel it now. His last bank statement said he had over $600,000 in cash in just that one account. What would $50,000 hurt?

"I've got a great idea!"

"Yes?"

"Go get my wallet."

Jumping up, I ran to my office to get his billfold but brought back the checkbook too. Since I'd been doing all his finances for the past couple of years, he probably forgot that there wasn't a lot of extra dough in the leather folds.

"Got it, Dad!"

"Okay, this is what you do. There's a $20 in there, right?"

"Yeah?"

"I want you to take that and go buy a book by Suze Orman. She's got some amazing tips on how to manage your money."

"Huh?"

"You never want to listen to me. Maybe reading her books will help."

Are you kidding me? I have to read a book? Can't you just write me a check?

Desperately trying not to show my disappointment, I put my hands in my pockets and grabbed my thighs. Sure, I was raised to figure things out on my own, and for most of my life put me in good stead, but how I wished, just for once, that someone would take care of me.

"Okay, Dad. I'll get onto that next time I go to Borders to buy you more books on tape," I replied with a sigh. *When I spend my own money buying you more tapes your $400 won't cover.*

"That's my girl. I know you can figure it out. You'll be just fine."

Walking back to my office, I wanted to kick a few walls along the way. I had some huge bills coming. The mortgage alone was over $5,000 a month.

Opening his checkbook, I stared at the ginormous amount of money sitting in his account and wondered how I could siphon a few bucks off the top. He'd never see the statement. I could just lie to him and mentally add back in what I took when we reconciled it at the end of the month.

But his bean-counting mind always knew exactly what should be on the bottom line every month, and with my propensity for screwing up math problems, I knew I'd get busted big time. I never had a good poker face.

Just as I was feeling defeated, the light bulb in my brain lit up.

Oh my God! I forgot I have an equity line on the house. If my money runs out, I'll dive into that.

Despite the fact I was pissed at him, I had renewed hope that everything would work out. I didn't need some financial wizard telling me how to run my life. I would be all right, thank you very much.

Entering his room one last time to make sure he was covered up properly and that his music was still on, I saw him fast asleep, apparently worn out from our discussion. I couldn't help but smile. He probably knew exactly what I was aiming for, but unless I came right out with what I wanted, he never bit the bait—not when I was young and certainly not now. He believed in my ability to find a way on my own.

Leaning over to kiss him one last time, I found myself ashamed that I had gotten myself into this money mess at all. Maybe if I stopped being such a little Spendy Wendy with frivolous things for my kids, I'd have more money to spend on him.

I needed to get back to that woman who couldn't wait for him to move in. This journey we were on was going to take time—his time—and I didn't want to look back on any of it with anger.

CHAPTER 16

Love Revelation

"Dad, what's that lump on your lip?" I asked the following morning as I watched him suck on a piece of pineapple. "Does that make it hard to chew?"

Moving the fruit to the other side of his mouth, he masticated the morsel until it was mash before swallowing. Nodding with a scowl, he confirmed that it was painful.

While my father never wore a bathing suit in his life—why would you if you don't know how to swim—skin cancer still found a way to plant its seed and grow over time. The proof was already on his arms. After years of working in the yard in a short sleeve shirt, thick, dry skin lesions covered his body. Now, an equally ugly crater was erupting inside his lip.

"Dad, I think we need to have that looked at," I instructed, moving in closer for a better look.

"No, just leave it alone," he grumbled, gesturing for Enemi to feed him his oatmeal. "I hate going to doctors."

"I know, but you keep biting it when you eat. Wouldn't it be nice to have it gone?"

Sucking down the soft cereal, he thought for a moment. "It's been hurting for a long time."

"I know just the doctor to take you to. You're going to love him," I happily announced, coming from a place of experience. In my youth, I thoroughly enjoyed the sensation of the sun's rays all over my nearly naked body. By the age of thirty-two, I saw my dermatologist on a regular basis, as he cut, burned, and examined every inch of my now leathery hide.

"Tell you what—I'll make the call right now."

The following day, we loaded Dad in the car for what I thought would be a quick visit, only to find doctors are all alike. Once again, the wait time was insufferable.

"My body is killing me," he said, squirming to find a more comfortable position in his wheelchair. "Let's go home."

"We're here now. Let's see this through," I answered, wiping the drool from the corner of his mouth that formed when he'd been asleep for too long or was about to hyperventilate.

"Mr. Madden? Mr. Madden?" a cute nurse with bright green eyes called. Holding a clipboard with his name on it to her chest, she said, "It's your turn."

"Okay. That's us!" I cheered. "Get ready to be impressed."

Wheeling him into the room myself, I instructed Enemi to take a walk. I wanted time alone with my father, especially if the news wasn't good.

"Do you think he'll be long? I get so angry that these doctors think we have nothing better to do than sit and wait around for them," Dad bellowed.

But before I could say, "Want a drink of water?" Dr. Menkes walked in.

"Hi, Mr. Madden. What seems to be the problem today?"

Without saying a word, Dad just pointed to his lip.

Putting on magnifying glasses, Dr. Menkes, a maturing man of my generation, wheeled his stool up.

"It's a squamous cancer lesion," he announced as if it were a mere spider bite.

"Is that bad?" I asked. It sounded bad.

"Well, it's cancer and if left untreated will continue to grow."

Poking his nose in ever closer, studying the specimen, he reassured, "Mr. Madden, you won't die from it, but it needs to come off."

Remembering how I'd had several thick buggers cut off my skin, I was fearful of what "come off" meant.

"Can you freeze it?" I questioned, noticing my father begin to sink into his quiet place.

"No, we'll have to cut it off. I'll have to go inside his mouth, start deep and remove half his lip."

Horrified, I instantly envisioned my handsome father sitting in his recliner for the rest of his life with a piece of his face missing.

"Cut it off? I don't think so," I blurted loud enough to make a nurse come running in to see if everything was all right. "You're not cutting into my father's face. He's ninety-six, for God's sake. There has to be a better way for him to be comfortable! Can't you just numb it, so it won't hurt if he bites into it?"

Realizing that my cheeks were burning red (and not because of my rosacea) and I was about to lose it, Dr. Menkes sat back and thought for a moment. "Hmm, maybe we can radiate it."

Remembering how a girlfriend had recently been handed the scarlet letter C on her breast and how radiation became the means to treat it with high-energy waves that killed the tumor but did little damage to the rest of her body, I became excited.

"That's perfect! Please, find out if that will work."

He left to make a quick phone call as we sat quietly, holding each other's hands, fearful of what the outcome would be.

Before long, Dr. Menkes re-entered the room with good news. "I didn't know this, but apparently radiation is used all the time on the face because it can save the healthy cells and tissue without any scarring. I'll write you up a prescription. The oncology center is just around the corner on South Drive."

"Dad, isn't that great?" I said, cupping his face in my hands. "They won't be cutting your lip."

In true Jack Madden fashion, there was little emotion, just a nod of his head and a polite smile.

"Jack, you'll need treatments every day for six weeks."

Now it was Dad's turn to be heard. "Every day! How long do they take?

Readjusting his wire spectacles, the kind doctor studied my father, then me, and reassured us as if it were nothing. "Only ten minutes."

It was hard enough getting him to regular doctor visits every so often. Monday through Friday for six weeks would be torture.

I saw my life going down the tubes with this daily inconvenience.

When we arrived home an hour later, Enemi transferred Dad to his chair. It was only 1:00 p.m. and too early for bed, but I could tell by the droopy look in his eyes that he'd be asleep for the rest of the afternoon.

Getting ready to go back to the office, I bent over to kiss him.

"Honey," he said, opening his eyes. "I want you to try to get out more at night. You've been locked up for too long. Please make arrangements to see your friends. You can ask Elizabeth to come. I like her too! Did you know she sings to me? We even pray together. I'll be fine."

Smiling at his consideration, I patted his cheek and said I'd try, but wondered where I'd go. All my friends were busy with their husbands and grandchildren.

It would be nice to go on a date, I mulled. *It's been well over a year since I had one of those.*

But since there were no guys in the wings waiting to take me out, I decided to resort again to that new age way of introductions: Match.com.

Later that evening, after getting him settled for the night, I climbed into bed with what had become the only warm body I'd slept with in years, my computer, and logged on. In the years after my divorce, I expected to use this site to find my true love, only to be highly disappointed. For whatever reason, the only guys that came sniffing also came with issues: alcohol, wife hating, children that hated them, or a lack of money and want to spend mine. But it'd been six years since I last tried. Maybe they all had received a little therapy and were ready for a real relationship.

Let's see if my old profile is still in here, I thought as I logged on.

Pulling it up, I changed the wording to reflect what I was currently doing and updated the photos. It took me all of ten minutes and then I was launched.

Okay! Bring on the men. I chuckled, hoping this time, things would be a little different. Before I knew it, the "likes," "winks," and "favorites" came flying through cyberspace.

Doesn't anyone send a note to introduce themselves anymore? I complained, sadly realizing the game hadn't changed. *As if you telling me you "like" me is going to get me excited. I know nothing about you.*

Then, just as I was about to turn off the light, it happened! A decent-looking guy (with his teeth still intact), geographically desirable (not on the other side of the world), who could not only spell but was prolific with his words, reached out.

"I read your profile and loved your photos. I think we have a lot in common. Would you like to meet for a drink?"

"Great!" I yelled as I responded with a hearty, "Yes! How about this Thursday?"

The date was set. I had three days to highlight my hair, get my nails done, and go shopping for a new outfit.

"I haven't had a date since grandpa moved in," I exclaimed to Lauren excitedly over the phone. "I don't think I even remember how to act."

My twenty-six-year-old laughed and informed me that dating was like riding a bike. You fall off, but, if you're brave, you get right back on again. "I'm so proud of you, Mom. I want to hear about it the minute it's over."

For the next couple of days, I thought about what to wear, how to act, and tried practicing stimulating conversation. Finally, the night came.

Taking a selfie, I texted my girls for their opinion on my appearance. Fortunately, all three gave the thumbs up, so off I went to my favorite watering hole in town, The Los Altos Grill.

Arriving five minutes early, I found him already sitting at the bar. He had saved me a seat.

Wow, a gentleman! And he's cuter than his picture! Could I get any luckier?

Saddling my fanny on the bar stool, I coyly asked, "Are you Ken? I'm Jackie." Before I knew it, we were two drinks in and deep in discussion of our lives, down to minute detail. All except one.

"So, you're a realtor. What else do you do with your days?"

I wondered if I should be completely honest and decided to let it all hang out.

"Well, my ninety-six-year-old father lives with me, so I spend a lot of time caring for him."

As he studied my face, I wondered if he were dissecting every pore and hair follicle like I was some lab experiment. I could not read his expression, so I couldn't tell if he thought this was good or bad.

I wondered if he heard me and should I tell him again?

Then, as if he'd changed the channel from a science documentary to a photo-finish high-stakes horse race, his eyes grew wide and his mouth dropped open.

"You're shitting me! You're taking care of your dad? I've never known anyone who's done that before."

"Yes, it was something I promised him long ago." Hoping to impress him with my altruistic nature.

Fiddling with his napkin, he downed his fresh drink in one swallow.

"That's to be admired, I guess. When do you think he'll die?"

"What?"

"Well, you said he was ninety-six. Do you think he'll leave soon? I mean, really, how long do these old people need? I bet he can't do anything for himself."

"Does that bother you?" I asked, swirling my wine in the glass but wanting to throw it in his face.

"It makes my sleeping over a little creepy, don't you think?"

Sleeping over? Who said anything about that? We just met.

"Hey, we could be right in the middle of something when he

decides he needs you. Kinda breaks the rhythm."

Seeing this Ken doll for all his plastic shallowness, I wanted off my stool and to drive away as fast as I could.

"So I take it you don't date women with children or elderly parents," I asked, surly.

Laughing, he ordered another drink, put his hand on my knee, and with an aggressive squeeze said, "Let's face it. None of us have a lot of time left, so I don't waste it on women I can't have sex with. Yep, no complications for me."

Sliding off the stool, I grabbed a $20 bill and threw it on the counter, wanting to call him every four-letter word in my arsenal but deciding to be a lady. Throwing my purse over my shoulder, I simply growled "Good luck" in disgust, and out I went.

Later that night, as I watched my father sleep, I began to study the face of the first man who ever loved me. He was perhaps the only man who ever truly loved me. I was thrown back in time to the very moment I knew how tethered we were to each other's hearts.

I think every woman remembers their first big romantic moments: the first flutter over a boy, the first kiss, the first real heartbreak. I was no different. When I was twelve years old, I thought the sun rose and set on a boy named Don—a black horn-rimmed specimen of acne, greasy hair, and crooked teeth. But to me, he was perfection. Surely he was the boy I'd marry one day.

Just as I traveled back to that age of innocence, Dad woke up.

"Hi, honey. Did you have a nice night out?"

Sitting on the chair next to him, I hoped he'd be up for a late night chat. I needed a real man to talk to.

"Dad, did I ever tell you about the first time I knew you loved me?"

Wiping the drool from the corners of his mouth, he looked up and smiled. "No, tell me."

"I was about three years old, so that would have made it 1955. Mom used to bundle me up in that quilted pink onesie and stick me in the sandbox to play while she got dinner ready."

"How you loved that sandbox." He grinned. "You could sit in it all day."

"It was late in the afternoon, and the wind was blowing all around me, messing up my castle. I remember getting frustrated, but then I looked up and you were at the gate to the yard just staring at me."

Closing his eyes, I could see he was trying to remember as well.

"I was? I was just standing there?"

I adjusted the blankets under his chin and took his hand through the safety bars of his bed.

"You weren't just standing there; you were smiling. I remember we just looked at each other for a minute or two. Then, you walked toward me, never saying a word, as I waved at you."

For a moment, we both sat in silence going back in time.

"I do remember," his mind now recalled. "You wanted me to play with you. But I didn't, did I?"

"No, you were still in your suit, so I imagined you didn't want it to get all messed up. But what you did was so much more special. You picked me up, despite me being covered in sand, and just held me. I can still feel how warm your cheek was next to my cold one."

"That's a sweet memory, honey. Thank you."

"I'll treasure it always because it was at that moment I understood love. Not all women get to feel that."

As his eyes grew heavy, I leaned to kiss him goodnight and thank him one more time.

"I'm one of the lucky ones, Dad. I love you."

CHAPTER 17

Evil Thoughts

What was supposed to only take six weeks of radiation turned into eight. Some lesions are stubborn and refuse the specific timeline to heal. Each day we made the trek to the oncologist where Dad, Enemi, and I would sit for several minutes in the waiting room before he was seen. To say the experience was excruciating for him doesn't begin to describe the torture his poor body endured as he was manhandled from the car to the wheel chair to the gurney for radiation and back again. Tired and in pain, sleep was the only way my father could survive the experience. And, sleep he did.

Since the dating debacle, I had decided to concentrate on more important things, like how to fall asleep at night despite the fact my body was bone tired. Unlike my father, it never failed—after a busy day of caring, I'd tumble into bed heavy-eyed only to find my mind was in overdrive. Most nights I got barely three hours unless I took a sleeping pill to knock me out.

"Mom, why don't you go to Tahoe?" Jenni asked, calling to check in on her fading mother. "It's June and you love it up there when the weather starts to get warm again. It might be the perfect break for you."

I sighed, thinking of our little piece of heaven right here on

Earth. How I'd love to run away and walk among the pine trees in the forest behind our Tahoe home. Having cabin fever there was such a different feeling than experiencing it in Los Altos. There, I expected it occasionally and let everything go, allowing the time for books, writing, or just staring out the window at the inclement weather holding me inside. But when it happened in my main residence, all I felt was trapped.

"There's no way I can get away right now," I said, closing my eyes and remembering the times I'd escape there after my divorce. Only there did I feel centered and at peace.

"Why not? Can't Enemi spend the weekend with him?"

Thinking back to several weeks before when the two of them were having a contest to see who could sleep the entire day away, I simply told my child, "I think she's on overload. She hasn't had a single day off in years. While she says she desperately needs the money, I can't do that to her."

"Well, how about getting with your girlfriends?"

"To be honest, I'm just not up for all that small talk. I feel like I have absolutely nothing to say."

As Jenni kept suggesting new ideas, I retorted with excuses. Soon a heavy pause lay between our sentences. Feeling defeated, she said goodbye. She had things to do, people to see, and places to go. She was young and living a rich, busy life. All my kids were. While I was grateful they were safe and happy, I envied their freedom. Deciding I needed to do something for me, I woke Enemi to let her know I was going for a walk and ended up crying in the park around the corner.

Sitting on a bench, I watched young mothers pushing their babies on the swings and was reminded of all the times I had done this with my own. When they became squirrely in the late afternoon, right before dinner and I wanted to wear them out so they'd fall asleep early, we'd go there and play. It was also where Timmy had his birthday parties because all he wanted to do was run around—no clowns or blow-up jumping structures, just one with the wind and his little friends. Instead of days of wine and roses, they were days of sand and shovels, soccer balls and softballs, and the rope swing across the creek.

Where did that time go? I sighed. *I was so happy then, and fulfilled. No one can ever say I didn't love being a mommy.*

Arriving home an hour later, I saw Enemi was preparing to leave. Dad was content in bed with his rosary and about to fall sound asleep.

"Are you leaving?" I asked, knowing the answer by the purse in her hand and the look on her face that said she was anxious to escape.

"Yes, I'll see you tomorrow. He's really tired today. I bet he sleeps through the night."

Preparing for another night of quiet nothing, I nodded my head and opened the door. "I'll see you tomorrow. Thank you."

Later that evening, Michelle called to check in. I was sure she'd been talking to Jenni because the litany of questions sounded awfully familiar.

"Mom, why don't you try to get out more?" Michelle encouraged her sad sack mother. "You've got those girls you can pay to stay with him. Call some friends and go out to dinner."

I sat quietly, thinking how lovely that sounded.

"You know, if you don't contact people, they might forget about you," she encouraged with her twenty-nine-year-old wisdom.

I feared they already had.

"Have you heard from Oliver?" Michelle asked, bringing up a name from the not-so-distant past.

While I understood that my girlfriends were busy with their lives, their husbands, and now their grandchildren, I could forgive that. At least they occasionally called to check in on me. But how could I forgive someone I'd been hanging out with for almost two years, someone I had introduced to my children and father, and someone I had invited for dinner at the holidays, only to have him vanish the minute my life took a different course?

"No, not a word. I guess he didn't want to get involved with all this."

"Have you reached out to him?"

Thinking of all the people I barely knew who sent a card or called to see how I was surviving, I said flatly, "What's the point? He's busy. Maybe he thinks I don't have the time."

"How would he know if you don't reach out?"

Feeling the effort was more than I could handle, but more fearful of another rejection because of my choice to care for my dad, I made some excuse and let it go.

After saying our goodbyes, I meandered through the house, aimlessly looking for something to keep me occupied while he snored. Going into the bathroom, I took one look in the mirror and wondered how much longer I could handle all this. There was no amount of makeup that would ever be able to cover the dark circles around my eyes. Since Dad had moved in, I went from being somewhat youthful at the age of fifty-eight to looking like an old hag at sixty. All I needed was a wart on the end of my chin and a few missing teeth, and I'd be in perfect costume for Halloween.

Entering his room, I proceeded to change his diaper, pushing the dead weight of his body in one direction, then the other, as he slept through. Suddenly, profound sadness washed over me. For some reason, Dad didn't want to talk like he did in the earlier days. I wanted to think it was because he was tired; he seemed to be sleeping more all the time. But I was worried that maybe he just didn't have anything left in him to say. No longer were there stories about his youth, how even at a young age he was the dutiful child taking on odd jobs to bring whatever pennies he could back to the family piggybank. He also seemed disinterested in what his grandchildren were up to or how I was doing in my job.

How I missed hearing about how smart the nuns and priests thought he was and how it was they who encouraged him to go on to higher education. Dad was the first in his family to go to college. It was never a burning ambition. In fact, he had never given it much thought, but when religious authorities thought something was a good idea, he paid closer attention.

And then there were all his memories of watching his four children grow up. He held such pride in his heart over our accomplishments, whether it was learning to ride a bike for the first time or the fact that we occasionally got a math problem correct. The grin on his face over the simplest of successes always tugged at my heart. To him, we were perfection just as we were and he was proud that we turned out loving, moral human beings. Once, there wasn't a subject we didn't explore. Now all I heard was silence. Our time together had become my responsibility to his physical needs and I was on overload.

Perhaps I should have listened to all those people and put him in a home. The way he was going, I imagined he'd outlive me!

Standing over the snoring beast, I didn't just blubber, I raged over the unfairness of it all. Why was it always me that had to take care of people? Was this all some contract my soul had made before I arrived on this planet, and if so, why was I so stupid to sign up for it?

Steam that had been building inside poured out of every orifice in my body. I was tired, and I was becoming unglued with self-pity.

You've not only destroyed my house but my life! I'm a prisoner in the mess!

Jenni's bedroom, with walls that had been freshly painted a cheery yellow and the carpet newly shampooed, was now beginning to look much like my bedroom after my grandmother had her way with it. Stains covered the carpet, from spilled food to debris that had escaped his diapers on their way to the garbage. Her dresser was covered with water stains from wet glasses, pill bottles lay scattered everywhere, and her curtains were destroyed!

How in the hell did they become so tangled? Did he play with them in the middle of the night trying to look outside?

Forcefully pulling up his blanket to tuck it under his chin, I noticed a stack of pillows in the corner, one right on top of the other. During the day, these served to elevate his head, his knees, even his feet. With my mind beyond tired—in fact, it was as fuzzy as a TV with no reception—it began to travel to a dark place. My humanity was faltering. Like the Sirens in Greek mythology calling to sailors so their ships would crash on the rocks, the pillows suddenly sang an evil song.

No one would ever suspect he was suffocated. He's 96 after all. People die in their sleep all the time. Plus, he's so tired, he won't even struggle for air.

Picking up an extra fluffy one, I stretched out the ends out as far as they'd go until the down inside was stiff, like a board covered in fabric. Walking over to his bed side, I held it high over his head. Just as I began to lower it, the reality of what I was doing slapped me across my heart with an invisible two-by-four.

"Oh my God! What am I thinking?" I cried aloud.

Horrified at myself, I threw the pillow across the room, fell to my knees, and burst into prayer.

"Please, dear Jesus. I need help! I can't do this by myself anymore. All this taking him to doctors is wearing all of us out," I sobbed. "Please, please don't let me wish him away. I know one day he'll be gone, and I'll want him back again."

Pulling myself together, I apologetically kissed his snoring face and left the room utterly mortified. I needed rescuing, but where to turn? Enemi was obviously just going through the motions. None of my friends had ever experienced something like this, so there was no one I could turn to for suggestions. Knowing I'd have to rely on something I'd grown to despise— the medical profession—I decided to talk to his doctor in the morning.

CHAPTER 18

A Time for Changes and Memories

"Hello. This is Rite Aid Pharmacy calling. The prescription you ordered cannot be filled without your doctor's consent. Please call the physician," I heard on the phone the following morning.

What the hell? It's cholesterol medicine. Why do we need to call the doctor? It's not like we're abusing Ambien or Oxycodone.

But as instructed, I called his physician.

"Hi, this is Jack Madden's daughter calling. His refill was denied, and we were told I had to call you."

"Let me check his records," replied a high-pitched, squeaky voice. "I'll get right back to you."

When did the doctor hire a seven-year-old as a receptionist? Either everyone's so much younger these days, or I'm just getting old, I thought.

Putting the phone on speaker so I could hear the minute she returned, I began catching up on chores. First, I scrubbed the kitchen sink, then the counters and sticky fingerprints off the cabinets. Still the elevator music played on.

Geez, they even make you wait on the phone.

Next, I swept the hardwood floor. And just when I was

about to fill the sink with hot water, I heard, "Hello? Are you still there?"

"I'm here. I've been here for twenty minutes."

"I'm sorry it took so long. I had a hard time finding his chart. He hasn't been in here in over three years."

"That's because he's so damn healthy," I said annoyed.

"It looks like the doctor needs to see him before she can prescribe anything."

"You mean I have to bring him in there?"

"Yes, we have an opening tomorrow."

"Please put the doctor on the phone," I hissed, desperately trying to keep my cool. "This just won't work for me."

A few minutes later I heard, "Hello, Miss Madden, this is Doctor Wong. What can I do for you?"

"Thank you for talking to me. I'm really struggling here. Every time Dad has an appointment he sleeps literally for days afterwards. He just finished eight weeks of radiation for cancer on his lip. Thank God it worked. He is now cancer-free, but I don't think he has the strength to come. Can't you just prescribe the same stuff again?"

Listening to all her medical reasons as to why it was important to see him, I wanted to break down and cry. The true reality was that it was I who didn't have the strength to keep doing this.

"There has to be a better way," I pleaded. "I recently read about hospice and how it's now about declining health and not just for the dying. Couldn't we set him up with that so people come to him?"

For a moment, there was silence on the other end of the phone. Then, with astounding affirmation, I heard, "You know, Miss

Madden, that's a great solution. I'll renew the prescription and send you some options so you can choose which organization you like."

"Really? That's terrific!" I happily replied, feeling like the troops were about to land at Normandy, and I'd be rescued from the hell I was living in.

Ten minutes later, the email arrived with her recommendations. Looking through them, I found one that spoke to me: Mission Hospice. The website looked friendly and I loved their philosophy: "A place for patients and families."

Especially for families. Sometimes we need it more than the patient!

I made the call and spoke with a friendly woman who said she'd come for a consultation the following day. Delighted, I hung up, but realized I now had a bigger problem: how was I going to tell Dad? In his world, hospice meant the grim reaper was hanging just outside the door, scythe firmly in hand. And he had no intentions of letting that demon in anytime soon.

Walking into his room, I saw he was awake.

"Hi, Dad. I'm so glad to see you're finally up."

Wiping the long wisps of white hair away from his eyes, I tried to summon the courage to tell him about my brilliant idea. Instead, I asked, "Want to hear your music while I get your breakfast ready?"

At his nod, I turned on his favorite CD and ran out the door. Enemi arrived shortly after and for the next few hours I found any and every excuse to avoid the conversation: folding laundry, taking the dog for a walk, watching reruns of Law and Order SUV, looking at my teeth in the mirror.

At lunchtime, the perfect opportunity arrived. He was now

in his chair. Taking a bite of a soft-boiled egg sandwich, he got a look of annoyance and said, "You know honey, I've been thinking. I don't ever want to go back to another doctor again. I'm glad the cancer's gone, but no more doctors."

Oh my! This is the perfect segue!

Taking my seat next to his chair, I spouted my brilliant idea.

"Guess what! You don't have to. I have a new plan."

Putting down his sandwich, he waited.

"I've organized for a hospice service to help us," I announced, sounding as if I'd just invented some miracle cream for all the new wrinkles on my face.

As I waited for what I hoped would be a happy response, I noticed his face turn to stone. Silence didn't just waft in the air but caused the entire room to stand still. Then, with the fury of a tornado, he cried, horrified, "Hospice! Am I dying? I don't feel like I am."

Placing my hand on his, I smiled.

"No, Dad. You're not dying. It's mostly for me. I just get a little nervous that I'm not caring for you properly."

Calming down, he popped that last remaining bite into his mouth. "Well, I'm not ready to go, you know. I want to live to one hundred."

"And I'm not ready for you to leave," I answered, actually meaning it.

"I know my parents are waiting, your mother is waiting, my sister and brother are waiting, but I'm not going," he announced again through a mouthful of food.

Smiling over his intense desire to live, despite the fact that he lived in a world of nothing where no one came to visit, no movies were watched on TV, nor did he read one of the historical novels he loved so dearly. I gently glided my fingers over his rosy cheeks and guided his face in my direction. "I just want to take the best care of you I can, and these people will be just a phone call away. They come to us. We never need to leave the house."

"I never have to get in the car again? Or sit in a waiting room for hours?"

"Nope, and you never have to pay for your diapers, medicine, or any of the other stuff we need to keep your skin clean. It's all paid for through your Medicare."

"Medicare pays for everything?" he said, surprised. Always looking for ways to save money, he was now on board.

"Yeah, Dad. The nurses and doctors will come to visit you, and it's all provided under Medicare."

His eyes twinkled and a broad smile appeared on his face. He was utterly pleased. As he leaned his head back, settling into his pillows, he shouted, "Bring them on!"

"This also means when you're ready, you won't die in a hospital. You'll be here with me."

With an even bigger smile, he got comfortable and closed his eyes again for another long nap.

The following day, the reserves arrived with all their ammunition, yanking this exhausted soldier out of her foxhole.

"Your father's in perfect health," said Mary, a simple-looking nurse with a humongous cross hanging from her neck. Apparently she'd been a nun in another life but continued to wear her amulet, most likely to ward off the evil spirits that love to hang around the sick and dying. "He just might make it to one hundred."

"Great!" I smiled, thinking I just might make it too.

A few hours later, in came a case of Depends, ointments, gauze, bath soap, and novelettes. Hundreds of dollars' worth of supplies, and all for free.

Soon after, the social worker, Tracie Pyers, arrived to talk about all the services Mission Hospice had to offer. There was the chaplain who could offer spiritual guidance in times of fear, support groups for me if I became utterly overwhelmed, books to read, music to listen to, and a kind voice on the other end of the phone any time I needed it.

As Tracie talked to my father, I could see my life was about to change for the better. Not only would I have people in my corner, but my clear-minded father would have other people to talk to besides his daughter. By now, I was sure I'd become rather boring since I never had anything new to say.

It wasn't long before Dad and Tracie were discussing the 49ers, Giants, and life in the city. With Tracy being a native San Franciscan too, the two of them talked their Catholic schooling, family, and politics. Dad was extra pleased to hear she was a Democrat. He had a new friend.

"So, what do you think?" I hoped he was as happy as I with our new situation.

"Oh, honey, this is great!"

"Good! You know they have someone who can talk to you about spirituality."

"No, I don't need that."

"It's free, remember. It might be nice to see what it's all about."

With thick eyebrows resting on the bridge of his nose, he grumbled.

"Dad, what's wrong? I thought you'd like something like that."

"I don't need anyone trying to convert me."

"He's not going to try to convert you, silly. But you might have some questions about life on the other side."

"No, Father Warwick and I covered all that."

For the next month, life continued, quiet, uneventful, orderly, but now with a happy peacefulness. The fear I had about loading him in the car all by myself in the middle of the night, like I often did with my mother, was over. Any issues that might occur could be solved with one phone call.

"Maybe I can do all this after all," I said to Lauren on her visit home to spend time with her grandfather.

"Mom, of course you can do this. But sometimes we all need a little help."

My world felt lighter. That's not to say the days weren't oppressively quiet and long, or that Enemi wasn't showing severe signs of overwintering. While I had my issues, she definitely had hers. As a mother of four, she'd lost all her boys: the oldest back to her native country, the second to a group home for emotional issues, and the baby to her now former husband. As for her daughter, she too was showing signs of mental illness. Because of her daughter's rages and violent outbursts, everyday Enemi was worried she may not see her child when she arrived home. It was hard to stay upset with her for I knew she was doing her best, but some days, in my opinion, her best just wasn't good enough.

There wasn't a day that went by that, at some point, I found her wrapped up in blankets hibernating like a bear in January. But knowing the troops were not far helped me to look the other way.

"Jackie, you're such a busy girl," Dad remarked as I threw in another load of laundry. I'd just taken out the trash, scrubbed the kitchen, and swept the floors. "From the time you were little, you've always been so busy."

"Really?" I asked as I began to fold the warm towels fresh from the dryer. Wanting to hear more about his perspective of his daughter growing up, I put the towels down and sat next to him. "I was just a kid, so I don't remember. I know I loved playing with my dolls. What else did I do?"

Patting my hand, he looked away to lasso the memories.

"You hardly sat still. You know, you never napped. How you drove your mother crazy." He shifted from side to side in his chair, looking like he was making a hole to hide in. "If you weren't mothering your dollies, you were skipping in the yard, climbing a tree, or dancing."

Pausing for a moment, an affectionate smile curled his lips. "How you loved to dance."

"I do remember that. And you were my favorite partner!"

Looking into his shining eyes, I recalled how I couldn't wait for him to get home so he could twirl me around the room like Fred did with Ginger, only my feet were glued on top of his. Standing at the picture window in the dining room, ready to perform in my white tutu and pink satin sash, I'd peer into the gray stillness of the day's fading light, tapping my ballet slipper impatiently.

"Every night I'd wait for you, and if you were the least bit late, there was hell to pay in the house." Fluffing the pillow behind his neck, I patted his cheek. "Mom hated it when you were late because I wouldn't stop bugging her."

With a rare belly laugh at the thought of his six-year-old child ranting for the music to begin, he agreed. "Yes, your mother could get cranky if I made you wait too long. Do you remember your first dance class?"

"Do I remember it? Absolutely! I sobbed the whole way there."

My mother thought ballet would be good for me. She knew I loved to dance because of the way I flitted and floated all over the house with scarves in my hands, beads around my neck, and flowers in my hair. It didn't matter if I had real music or a tune playing wildly in my head.

"Mom said ballet would give me good posture. I guess I was a little portly back then. All I ever heard her say was 'Jackie, stick your stomach in and stand up straight.'"

Remembering how I would have been much more adept at modern dance than ballet, I giggled. "I guess I was too much of a free spirit. Isadora Duncan and I would have been great dancing buddies with the way we both love interpretive movement."

"Yeah, that outfit your mother put you in was not your style. What was it? A black leotard and some pink tights? God, how you wailed."

"She made it worse by putting my hair in a tight bun. I recalled begging you to step in and save me." I roared with laughter.

"Do you remember who took you that day?" he asked, his grin widening.

"Do I? Yes, you! I think you had to pry my fingers off the car door to take me inside that dark hall at Notre Dame High School where the class was being held. You put my hand on the barre with the other little girls, and then left me!"

"Well, I didn't just leave you. First, I had to wipe your nose. How it was dripping." He chuckled. "But what you don't know is I went to the back of the room and hid to watch. I never left."

"Aw, that is so sweet. I didn't know."

For two years I struggled in that stupid dance class, hating every minute. Unlike the other little girls, I was beyond uncoordinated: my body wouldn't lend itself to the splits, backbends, or cartwheels. Being raised with brothers, I often felt wrestling was probably the better sport for me.

Finally, when I turned eight, I was granted a reprieve. Well, more like an expulsion. Excessive talking and ballet apparently aren't good dance partners, and I was released back into the wild.

"I've always marveled at how you did learn to dance. I can remember every Saturday your nose would be right up against the TV watching American Bandstand."

We hadn't reminisced like this in such a long time. Somehow the door to his memories had been pushed wide open, and it all came spilling out. I loved every minute.

"Ha! Then, I'd go into my room and practice with my door. I'd tie a rope around the knob and that would be my partner's arm. Funny to think that without any formal training I became a dance teacher. But I think it's time I gave it up."

Dad's eyes grew wide with astonishment as if I'd lost my mind. Shaking his head, he asked, "Why? You love teaching those kids."

"I know, but it's been twenty years and maybe it's time to give someone else the chance to take over. Besides, I can hardly get back up off the floor anymore. It's not good when a three-year-old has to help you up."

Truth be told, the cord that tied all the pieces of my life together was becoming dangerously frayed. With Enemi becoming more and more tired, I was picking up her slack. That, along with trying to sell homes, choreograph, teach, set up dancing venues for the kids to perform at, as well as putting together the year-end recital, I often felt like Humpty Dumpty about to crack into a million little pieces, and that I would never be whole again.

Later that evening, after his rosary, dinner, and pills, I could see he was in a pensive mood. Confused, since he had been jovial and happy earlier, I asked, "Are you okay?"

With foam dripping out of his mouth as he scrubbed away at the tartar on his teeth, he spat and asked sullenly, "Why would you want to quit? I don't understand."

"My body hurts all the time. Besides, I'm almost sixty. I think it would be better for them to have a younger teacher who was fresh."

Wiping his chin with the back of his hand, I could tell by the timid look on his face this was much deeper for him. Then he mumbled, "Is it because of me?"

While my father was deathly afraid of spending the end of his life in a nursing home, he was even more frightened to think he'd ever be a burden. In my youth, he definitely could be surly at times, cranky at others, even obstinate when he wasn't getting his way. But, from the moment he moved in, only once did I hear him complain, and it was over the usual—not wanting to spend extra money for his care. It was evident he was working hard on being the perfect house guest so as not to be evicted.

Taking his toothbrush, I wiped the rest of the drool away with a napkin, put his face in both my hands and reassured him. "Dad, no. Absolutely not!"

"But if I weren't here you wouldn't be so tired all the time."

"Don't you even go there! This is not about you. Sometimes

you just need to let go of things in your life so other things can enter."

As he started to yawn, I sensed he was worn out from all the stewing his brain had been doing. As I kissed him goodnight, he grabbed my hand and whispered, "I want to be there on your last day of class."

"You do?"

"Yes! You'll be having some sort of recital, won't you?"

"Yeah, but Dad, it will be long and crazy, and you'll have to sit in your wheelchair."

"I don't care. I want to be there. I was there when you started; I need to be there when you finish." Holding my hand tighter, he pulled me closer. "I want to be there for the full circle."

As I left him to go to sleep, I found myself thinking of all the times my father stood in the background so his family could shine. As we had grown to know each other more intimately over the last few years, I saw that despite the fact he lived his life quiet and humble, my dad had a healthy ego. He knew who he was, and his strengths and weaknesses, but he never bragged about any of his accomplishments. They were all just a matter of fact. He never wanted to bring any attention to himself.

Instead, the place of honor was reserved for those he loved. He felt no need to be the celebrity of any Madden Family Production. We were the superstars of his masterpiece theater.

Two weeks later, I hung up the tutu and ended my dance career. No longer would I be skipping around a room with feathers in my hair and glitter on my cheeks with twenty-five kindergartners. Gone were the days of neon leotards and gyrating moves with first and second graders. And never again would the world witness my hip-hop bounces, Zumba wiggles, or creative modern fluidity.

True to his word, and despite the fact he had to spend two hours sitting in that painful cage that could make him weep with discomfort, my father sat smiling, unable to see, in the midst of a couple hundred parents and grandparents cheering their tiny dancers on, with Jenni by his side. He had stood in the back of a dark room fifty-four years before to watch me begin, and now he was front and center to witness the end. One of many full circles in our life together was complete.

CHAPTER 19

Just the Way You Are

Like holidays and other good things in life, summer came and went with the speed of light. Autumn's colors of gold and red were popping everywhere. We were still living a world of routine, but it didn't bother me as much as before. I'd given up trying to have a personal life. It was just too much effort for no results. So I settled into the calm, especially knowing I had the support of hospice whenever I needed it. Even Enemi was cooperating by showing up on time and not racing out before her quitting time. Seeing all was right with the world, I decided I'd try to get away to my cabin for a couple of days.

I called my brother Tim and requested that he stay with our father. Once that was cleared, I prepared Dad.

"Hi, Dad," I sang, bringing in his mail one afternoon. "I'm going to Tahoe tomorrow for a couple of days."

Instantly, his face lit up. "That's terrific! It'll be good for you to get away. I know how much you love it up there."

"Thanks. Tim is coming down to stay. You'll get to have a nice visit."

He was beaming now. The thought of his once wild child taking the time out of his busy schedule obviously brought him joy.

"Good!" He nodded, the dimple in his chin deepening.

The following day, suitcase in hand, I found him at the breakfast table with his oatmeal, fruit, and pastry. Since living with me, I added extra sweets to his diet. After all, at ninety-six, what did it matter if he gained a few pounds? Enemi was strong enough to throw an elephant.

"Dad, I'm leaving in about an hour for Tahoe and Kim said she'd be here with you until Tim gets here. Enemi has an appointment she needs to go to."

Looking at his caregiver, he smiled and asked, "Do you get to do something fun too?"

Spooning another mouthful of oatmeal into his mouth, her gold toothed grin sparkled. "I'm going to see my son in San Rafael." This was her child who spent his days in a group home for emotionally challenged children. Enemi rarely was able to see him, so she was especially grateful for the time off.

Dad nodded his approval. "That will be nice for you."

"I'll be back later to get you into bed," she reassured.

Then, remembering which Kim I was talking about, my father asked, "Is that your friend with the spiky hair?"

"Yeah. She hasn't been here in over three months. Good memory."

Suddenly, a frown turned the fine lines on his forehead into crevices. He had something on his mind.

"What's wrong?"

"Nothing."

I sat next to him, thinking there was no way I could leave knowing he was feeling troubled.

"Dad, something's wrong. Don't you like Kim?"

"I don't think you should be friends with her."

Perplexed, I looked at him. How could he even say that?

He'd only met her once. Wondering where the hell this was coming from, I put my elbows on the table and rested my face in my hands to look into his eyes.

"Why would you say that? I could understand if she was a man. You've already made it perfectly clear men and I aren't allowed to spend time together. Remember? You told me I was done with dating."

He put his head down, studying his meal.

"I should never have said that," he said at last. "You're a young, pretty woman. You should try to date."

"Okay, then what is it?"

Swaying his shoulders back and forth, as if he was a dog battling fleas, he huffed and puffed until the reason finally came out.

"Is she? Is she, uh, a . . .?"

"Is she a what, a woman?"

Annoyed, he sat straight up, ready to make his point.

"I know she's a woman. But is she a real woman?"

I threw back my head and convulsed with laughter. "Are you asking if she's a lesbian?"

"Yeah, one of those."

Now, while my father was open to conversation about just about anything, he was still pretty old-school when it came to what the church said about what was right and what was wrong.

"You should be ashamed of yourself," I ribbed. "She's one of my best friends and, yes, she's gay."

"She might be after you."

Wanting to get him riled up, I teased, "And would that be so bad?"

Stunned, all he could say was, "I don't want you to change."

Grabbing his hand for reassurance, I told him he had nothing to worry about. I still liked men way too much. But always looking for a moment between the two of us, I decided not to drop the topic just yet. He may never be swayed when it came to politics, but humanity was a different story, even if the church he grew up with said it should be done another way.

"First of all, Kim is in a loving relationship with her partner. They've been together for many years. But let's talk about this."

Noticing his chin was glued to his chest, I knew I didn't have too much time to get my point across before he completely checked out.

"All my life I've had wonderful gay friends. People who have been there for me when no one else was," I said, placing my hand on his cheek. "Let me ask you—do you think someone wakes up one day and says to themselves, 'I think I'll change my orientation from straight to gay today'? No, they don't."

He glanced up as I continued.

"They were born that way. And didn't God create us all in His image? If you believe that like you say you do, then it doesn't matter what sexual persuasion we are. It also doesn't matter if we're white, black, brown, green, or purple."

He was now looking up, softening as my point hit home.

"Do you remember when we were little, how you and Mom stressed that we should love everyone?"

When he nodded, I went in for the kill.

"Even when those black girls beat me up at camp when I was eleven and I wanted to hate all black people, you said that they did a bad thing, but not everyone was like them. That I should forgive and accept."

Thinking for a moment, a thread of a smile crossed his lips.

"And, besides, the church has changed its stance on the gay community. They're welcome to come to Mass and receive the sacraments now. It's become inclusive for all."

"You're right, honey. That was stupid of me. She's nice and I'm glad she's been a good friend to you, but I like you the way you are. I guess I just got nervous for a minute."

Kissing his cheek, I stood up to grab my suitcase, but before I could leave, he asked, "Do you remember the first time I took you to the Stations of the Cross? I think you were only five."

How I remembered. It was in the evening and the church was lit mainly by candlelight. I'm sure I nagged him into letting me come along because I always wanted to go where he went, but since I'd yet to have any true religious training, I found myself confused.

Placing me in a pew in the front, he told me to stay put while he prayed before the fourteens pictures of the agony Christ endured.

"Yes, how could I forget? I couldn't understand why you were bowing in front of pictures of a half-naked man."

"I told you to sit there, but you crawled out and stood alongside me the entire time." He grinned at the memory. "You were so cute. You kept asking me a million questions."

"Well, you have to admit, the story of a father wanting his son to die for sins other people created was a little scary. I was afraid I might do something to make you really mad and you'd want me to die too."

Rubbing his chin with his thumb and index finger, he began to giggle.

"It took a lot of convincing with you. You always had questions when it came to religion. You were like your mother in that way. You know when we first got married, she wasn't a very good Catholic."

"Really?" I said, surprised. "You mean she didn't buy into all the nonsense too?"

"No, I had to do a lot of convincing."

Smiling, he went quiet for a moment.

"But as the years went by, she found so much solace in her faith."

In my childhood home, the only acceptable education was parochial, and I suffered all the rules: Skirts had to hit just at the knee, and if there was any question, the nuns sent us down on our knees to be sure the hem dusted the floor. Excessive chattering left me with my favorite solution for any mishap in our home—electrical tape—securely slapped across my mouth. And, if there was even a hint of a chance that you missed Mass over the weekend, you became the nun's whipping girl or boy as an example of impure behavior.

We were taught not just what to believe, but how to think. Feeling like a butterfly inside a dark box, I rebelled in my college years.

"I bet it made you sad when I stopped going to church when I was at USF."

He confirmed my assumption with a nod, but said he felt better knowing my rosary still sat next to my bed if I wanted to pray.

"I know that bothered you, Dad, and I'm sorry. But it was the 1970s and everyone was angry in the world. I was so afraid David would be sent off to the Vietnam War. I needed to blame someone for all the world's troubles, so God became my target."

"I understand. It's good to have a questioning mind. It's the key to powerful thinking."

Looking at the clock, I realized an hour had passed and I should hit the road. Putting my arms around my father's neck, I kissed his cheek, and reminded him, "I love you."

At that moment, Kim walked in smiling. "Hi Jack, how are you today?"

With an equally bright grin, he said to me, "I love you too. You're perfect just the way you are."

CHAPTER 20

Learning to Walk Again

Just as quickly as the roller coaster had taken me to the top, it began to speed down toward another obstacle.

"The one thing I want to do before I die is walk to the front door," Dad proclaimed, as if it were an ordinary request that could easily be bought at Target. "I want to get in the car and take you to the commissary one last time."

Listening to his desire, my heart sank. My father hadn't moved his legs in nearly four years.

"Dad, what a great wish to have," I said, looking into his bright eyes but afraid of how I was going to tell him that this was impossible.

"It's not just a wish. I know I can do it," he announced with resolve.

By the imploring look in his Irish eyes, this wasn't just some daydream of wishful thinking. There was a burning desire deep within his core to maneuver his legs one last time, take me to the Moffett Field Military base, and go shopping at the PX. As a retired naval captain in the Reserves, he still had access to the base. It was an outing we loved to do together in days gone by.

Wanting to change the subject, I tried to divert his attention to the Giants' season.

"That was some game last night, wasn't it?" I began. "They just might make it to the World Series again this year."

"Do you think you and Enemi could help me stand so I could try to take a few steps?"

"Boy, that Tim Lincecum is an incredible pitcher. I wonder how long his tiny body will be able to throw like that."

"I bet if you stood on one side of me and Enemi on the other, I could do it."

"I think there's a game on tonight too."

As I started to cover up his frail, broken body, Dad grabbed my arm, and stared imploringly, his eyes burning laser rays through me.

"Jackie, please. I know what you're doing here. You don't want to talk about this because you don't think I can do it. I need you to believe in me. I know I can."

My father was born with dominant genes of optimism and gratitude. Even in the darkest times, he found a way to believe all would be okay. While I sometimes wondered if he lived in a world of denial, rather than facing what was really in front of him, his doctor once told me he actually lived in a world of hope. Maybe that's why he had outlived everyone.

Bending over to kiss his forehead, I said, "Let me think about how I can make this happen for you."

"You promise you'll try?"

"Yes, Dad, I promise."

An hour later, I was hiking with my friend of over twenty years, Libby. Not only was she a licensed counselor, but she often knew the inner workings of my soul better than I did.

"I wasn't prepared for what all this was going to entail," I grumbled. "It's hard enough just tending to the day-to-day shit, and I don't mean that just figuratively."

Feeling the lovely summer air tickle my hair and the sun's warmth caress my shoulders, I was happy for the momentary reprieve. Nature had a way of giving me hope.

"I wish there was a training manual for caring for your parents. I'm sure there must be, but I think I'm too deep in the process now for one to do any good. I've had to learn what to do for him by the seat of my fat pants."

Stopping under a tree for some shade, Libby said encouragingly, "You're doing a great job. Stop being so hard on yourself."

"No, I'm not. If I were doing a great job, I wouldn't be hating my life right now. Everywhere I look I'm reminded of how much things have changed."

"Like what?"

"The house has been destroyed by his wheelchair. Every time Enemi or I move him someplace, another chunk gets knocked off a wall. The floor is covered in scratches, and the house smells. God, how it smells," I answered curtly, kicking at the dirt under my feet. "I throw his diapers out the minute he's changed, but it's like a musty, yeasty smell has been painted into the walls. Like gas that won't waft away."

As Libby put her arms around me, I burst into tears. "I'm beginning to hate it all again. I hate Enemi in my house every day. I hate that my brothers are so far away. I hate him for getting old. I hate me for hating."

Libby let me wail. For what felt like an hour, she lovingly patted my back until the heaving sobs turned into whimpers. Hearing a calm return to my breathing, she held me at arms-length, looked deep into my eyes, and instructed, "Maybe you can find something that will take his mind off of how his life is. What do you think would be a fun thing for him?"

"Funny you should say that. He wants to learn to walk again."

Her big brown eyes widened in surprise. "That's it!" Libby exclaimed. "Just find a way to help him believe he can walk again."

"How in the hell do I do that?"

Her eyes watched the clouds drifting overhead as she thought for a moment. "Well, he hasn't exercised in years, right?"

"Yeah."

"The first step to any physical activity is using the muscles. Maybe you could get a physical therapist to come to the house?"

Realizing at this point in his life it was more about the effort than the end result, I went home with a plan.

"Hi, Dad!" I called entering the family room. As always, he was in his natural position with his eyes closed, hand resting on his cheek as he relived some far away memory. "If you want to walk again, what you need to get your muscles strong is a physical therapist. I'm going to make a few calls."

Opening his eyes, he beamed and nodded. "When can we start?"

Kissing his cheek, I wondered where in the hell I could find a physical therapist who would work for free? The miser in my father hated paying for services, and this Mother Hubbard's cupboard was bare of any discretionary funds. But I knew there had to be a way. Then, the perfect solution came to me.

"Jenny, I've got an idea that might help both of us," I said excitedly, bumping into my friend later that day at the YMCA.

Jenny Nappo was a physical therapist taking time off to raise her two beautiful little girls, Taylor and Courtenay. Knowing I might be able to barter something with her, like the use of my cabin in Tahoe anytime her family wanted to use it, I said, "Dad says he wants to walk again. There's no way that will ever happen, but he has so little to look forward to that I thought it might lift his spirits just to try."

After I explained the situation about his crippled nature but determined constitution, she paused at first. "Jackie, how often does he want to be worked with?"

"It can be whatever you're able to give. I'll play with the girls while you do it so you don't have to make arrangements for them."

"How about on Thursdays at 11:30 a.m.? The kids are in summer school. Will that work?"

I was ecstatic.

Two days later, Jenny arrived with her endearing disposition and what Dad thought were strong Irish genes.

"Hi Jack." She beamed as I introduced the two of them. "I hear you want to walk. Well then, let's get you strong so it can happen."

She recited all the equipment she'd need: 2 lb. weights, exercise bands, and his walker. I immediately went to gather the tools of the trade so they could get started.

At first, there was no standing, let alone trying to walk. His legs had not just gone to sleep, they'd atrophied. There was work to be done to wake up the dead muscles and cells traversing through his mangled frame.

Weeks trickled by as she showed him the proper technique of doing bicep curls, side raises, and an over-head press with his functioning hand. The other side of his body just sat and watched.

"That's great, Jack!" Jenny cheered. "You're up to twenty repetitions."

While he did numerous leg extensions with his good leg, it was torture watching him try to get the damaged one even an inch off the ground. Finally, after a month, Jenny asked, "How would you like to try to stand today?"

Smiling, he glowed as if he'd just been asked to dance by the prettiest girl in the room. But there was no way he'd be able to stand on his own.

With Enemi and Jenny flanking his sides, they held his walker in front of him for security while keeping his recliner close behind.

"Okay, Jack," Jenny cheered. "Are you ready to try?"

He nodded with determination.

The two women grabbed the utility belt around his midsection and, with a count of one-two-three, he shot up with momentum. His good hand held on to the walker while they kept him erect. Then, they began pushing the wheels of the walker and kicking his bad leg forward.

"Great, Jack! You took three steps," Jenny exclaimed.

But as quickly as his smile had appeared, it dissolved as exhaustion reared its ugly head.

"I need to sit down," he sputtered, his body teetering. Grabbing the chair, Jenny pulled it behind him and Dad plopped down.

Throwing her arms around his neck, she kissed his cheek. "That was fabulous."

Shaking his head, he uttered in discouragement, "But I want to get to the door."

"Don't be so hard on yourself. This was your first time and look what you did!"

It was true he managed to move about five inches, but at this rate, it would take him all year to get halfway there. Maybe a year he didn't have left on his calendar.

Despite the encouragement and love from Jenny, Enemi, and myself, the scowl on his face showed he was obviously disheartened.

"That was terrible. I want to go to bed."

My heart crumbled as I felt saddened to think there'd be nothing in his final years that brought him any joy.

"Okay, Dad. We can try again another time."

Taking him to his room, despite the fact it was only noon, Enemi got him ready for bed. He proceeded to sleep for the next two days.

"I'm sorry, Jenny," I apologized as I walked her to her car. "I totally understand if you want to stop coming. He can get a little grumpy sometimes."

"Jackie, I adore your dad. Let's keep doing this. He did well," she reassured me as she rubbed my arm for comfort. "Two weeks ago he wouldn't have been able to take even one step. I'll be back next week."

Hugging her goodbye, I went back into the house, stood at the door to his room, and watched him nap. How I wished I could make things better for him. It seemed no matter what I tried: the books on tape, headphones attached to the TV so he could hear his Mass, or extra sweet treats were only Band-Aids healing the wounds of aging. Just a temporary solution. I wished that life had treated him better and that my mom was still here. She wasn't supposed to die first. I wasn't supposed to be in this predicament of giving up my life to take care of him.

A couple of days later, I prepared myself for the silence that would follow when he finally woke up. Whenever Dad felt truly defeated, he'd fall into a funk that took days to climb out of.

Finally, the sleeping prince awakened.

"Hi, Dad," I said, in a welcoming tone as I entered his bedroom. "Would you like to listen to your music before Enemi gets here?"

Turning his face towards me, I was surprised to see his face actually beaming.

"Can Jenny come today?"

Shocked at his happy mood, I asked, "Do you want to try to walk again?"

He nodded and I pulled up a chair to sit beside him.

"Dad, she needs to take care of her kids today."

"I know, but I'd love to see her again. She doesn't have to work with me. Just visit."

"You like her, don't you?"

"I love hearing about her kids and her husband. She's such a sweet girl. Do you know she's from Canada? I've never known anyone from there before. But the best part is that she's Irish too!"

"You like having someone to talk to. I must get pretty boring all the time," I asked, gently rubbing the morning stubble on his cheeks.

Looking back out the window, he hesitated before answering. Then, with a voice filled with loneliness, he answered, "I miss your mother."

Tears burning my eyes, I agreed. "Yes, I know. I miss her too."

And so it was. For the next couple of months, Jenny came with her fresh face full of love for him, and he for her. While there was some exercising going on, for the most part it was just talking. Dad was relearning the art of conversation, something that had died in him with my mother's passing.

It's been said that when the student is ready, the teacher appears. I'd been searching for the reason why my father was still alive. After all, everything had been stripped away and I couldn't see the value in just lying around all day with nothing to do.

But as I watched him come alive in those weeks with Jenny, I came to fully understand that the gift he was blessed with was hope. Hope ends fear. Hope brings courage. Hope is love, and love can make anything possible, even walking again. How I longed to be just like him, sharing his hope.

CHAPTER 21

Changing of the Guard

Fatigue is something we all feel from time to time. But caregiver fatigue is different. It's like plugging your cell phone in all night only to find the battery is still dead in the morning. No amount of sleep can recharge the individual.

God! She's out like a light again.

"Enemi," I called, shaking her shoulder. "Enemi, wake up."

Lifting her head, she slowly opened her eyes.

"Why don't you go out for some fresh air? I'm here to read Dad his mail. I will be here for about an hour."

Looking up with tired eyes, she stared at me for a moment with a glazed expression as if she were struggling to comprehend what I'd just said. Cobwebs tend to multiply in the brain when not exercised regularly. And, just like a sow bug rolled up into a ball in a child's hand, she slowly uncurled her body to muster all her strength to stand up.

"Thank you, Jackie. That's a good idea. I could use a walk. I'm really tired today."

"I know these days must be long for you. It's beautiful outside."

Finding my father in the family room, I thought about how things had declined. Enemi used to be so attentive, ready to take on any job when it came to his care. Now, she was that adorable dwarf Sleepy, always droopy-eyed and ready to fall asleep at any given moment, only this Snow White was losing her patience.

"Hi, Dad. I have your mail," I announced. "Are you ready?"

"Where's Enemi?" he asked.

"I told her to take a walk. Why?"

"I feel like she goes missing the minute she puts me in this chair. I call her, but she doesn't answer."

"I'll talk to her."

Things were apparently slipping through the cracks more than I thought. He'd never complained about her whereabouts before.

I went back to work and arrived home at 3:00 p.m. prepared to have a little come-to-Jesus meeting with her.

"Enemi, this isn't working," I said with deep concern in my voice. "I know you're tired. It's nice to know hospice is in the wings, but we still have to do the work. You've got caregiver fatigue, and, believe me, I understand because I feel it too. The only difference is that you're getting paid, and I'm not. "

Gazing expressionlessly at me with her chocolate-colored eyes, I wondered if we were truly connecting. With no response, I continued. "I've lessened your work hours, plus I give you time off during the day to run errands or to take a walk. We need to figure out how to make this better for all of us."

Suddenly, a look of horror crossed her face.

"Am I losing my job?"

"No, but this is how it needs to be going forward," I informed in my most boss-like manner. "I'll do everything from now on.

I'll even have his breakfast ready for you when you come so you won't have to deal with that too. All you have to do is be sure he's clean and dry, feed him his breakfast, and come when he calls you."

Faintly smiling, relief washed over her face.

"Okay, Jackie. I understand."

"We have to work together as a team," I repeated. "This is a big job, a tiring and boring job. But he deserves to have the best care we can give him."

Standing to give me a hug, Enemi squeezed me with her massive arms.

"Thank you, Jackie. I'll do my best."

And for the next couple of weeks, she did. She arrived on time, the laundry was washed and folded the very same day, and Dad's every need was attended to. But by week three, things went back to the way they were before.

Looking at my watch, I tapped my toe with anger. It was 9:45 a.m. and I was late for an appointment.

"Where is she?" I ranted to myself, looking out the window. "I told her I had a meeting this morning. I'm already late."

Twenty more minutes ticked away as fury raged through my body.

"Jackie!" my father yelled.

"Dad, I'm right here," I called, running into the room. Dad clearly wanted to be cleaned and have breakfast, but I couldn't move him.

"I want to get up."

"I know, but she's not here yet."

"Where is she?"

"I don't know. She's late and not answering her phone."

Harrumphing, he blew an exasperated sigh, and then hissed, "She takes such advantage. She always did."

Seeing his frustration, I remembered all the times she'd missed the mark when he was living in his own home: cooking for her village, the laundry that never ended, and the endless parade of cousins.

"Dad, I know you like her because she's cheap, but maybe it's time to hire someone we can truly trust."

Shaking his head, he said, "No, no, no. Just let it be."

"But this is now affecting me. I'm late for my appointment."

Looking up, his face went soft as the reality became clearer. "Just leave me here and go."

"I can't do that."

Just then, the front door swung open.

Running to meet her, my eyes shot bullets onto her contrite face.

"I'm so sorry. Traffic was horrible."

"Traffic is never so bad that it takes an hour to get here from your house. Did you leave late?"

Seeing she was busted, she admitted she had overslept.

Christ, how much sleep does one person need?

"I'm late for a meeting," I informed her as I grabbed my bag and ran for the door. "Dad is ready to get up."

This is not working, I thought to myself. But then I remembered how sweet she could be. She was a woman who loved everyone and always did try her best. Still, I needed to figure out a plan B. She was tired and becoming increasingly unreliable.

Arriving at the office for the meeting I'd now missed, I picked up the morning newspaper. As if the angels of caregiving heaven were guiding my angry hands, I turned straight to the full-page ad of Home Care Assistance.

Available 24/7. High caliber caregivers. No long-term contracts. Peace of mind.

The last item, "peace of mind," was like a relaxing melody from one of my meditation CDs: calm, sweet, and soothing. But it was the "no long-term contract" that also caught my eye.

Picking up the phone, I made the call to Home Care Assistance and was greeted by a lovely sounding woman who introduced herself as Lisa Mitzel.

"How can I help you?" she inquired.

With a sigh, I began our tale of caregiving woe and explained how Enemi needed a break.

Ten minutes later, I had the scoop. The minimum was four hours a day. While the rates were higher than what we paid Enemi, they'd come whenever we needed, even during the night.

Signing off, I thanked Lisa but informed her I was just gathering information for now. Little did I know I'd be calling her sooner than I thought.

The following day, I decided I needed a break. "Enemi, I'm going to Tahoe tomorrow," I announced. "My brother David will come down to spend a few nights with Dad while I'm gone. He doesn't know how to change his diapers, so you need to be here on time to help him."

Searching for a light behind her tired eyes, I asked, "Okay?"

"Yes, Jackie. I'll be sure Dave is taken care of."

"No, it's Dad that needs the help. Dave just needs to be shown how."

Leaving at midday for a four-day reprieve, the three-and-a-half-hour drive began peacefully enough, but halfway there, I found myself in a waterfall of tears.

I thought when we got hospice everything would be easier. After arriving at the cabin, I lay down on the couch once

I finished unpacking at 5:00 p.m., wrapped myself in a thick, fluffy blanket and closed my eyes. I awoke seventeen hours later when the phone jarred me awake.

"Jackie, what time does Enemi come?" Dave asked, confused.

Looking at the clock, it was now almost 10:00 a.m. Dad would need canoe paddles to work his way out of his soggy diaper at this point.

"What do you mean, what time is she supposed to be there?" I mumbled, still half asleep. "She should have been there an hour ago."

"Well, she hasn't shown up and she's not answering her phone."

Again?

Telling him about my new find in the newspaper, I said, "I'll call Home Care Assistance and see if someone can come out until we can figure this out. I'll keep trying her."

After no luck reaching Enemi, I made the call and heard Lisa's sweet voice again.

"Oh my God!" I exclaimed. "Our caregiver never showed up and my brother's stranded. Is it possible to get someone out there today?"

Pausing for a moment, she shuffled through her papers, then responded with a resounding, "Yes! We have a new hire. We'll get right over."

We've all heard that God works in mysterious ways. But He also creates miracles. As it turned out, Enemi had been in the hospital all night. She had kicked a metal gate and had to get several stitches on the bottom of her foot. Her cell phone had gone dead, and she didn't have our phone numbers written down in her wallet or purse.

To save the day, the Almighty Lord (and Lisa) sent Emori Suevdre (also known as Junior), a six-foot, 300 pound Samoan who sweetly resembled the character Shrek, on the wings of Archangel Michael. Not only would he become the light our family needed, but also the caregiver Dad deserved.

"Jackie, I can't tell you the difference in not only Dad's care today, but his attitude," Dave sang later. "I think we should try to keep him."

"He's that good, huh?"

"Really, he's amazing."

I looked out the window at the forest of pine trees across the way, I began to whimper—how I wanted to stay for the four days I had planned, but knew I better get home.

"Okay, I'll be back tomorrow and I'll talk to Dad. Thanks for giving me this little break. It was nice to get away."

The following day, I arrived to find my father doing all kinds of exercises as Junior called out the moves like a drill sergeant conducting boot camp.

"Okay, Jack! Again, lift that arm higher. Don't let the weight drop," he barked. Next, pointing to a space in mid-air for my father to kick his leg, he commanded, "See if you can hit my hand."

In the corner, David stood giggling. Sneaking up behind him, I whispered, "What the hell is going on?"

Turning with a grin as big as any I'd seen on Christmas morning, my brother laughed. "He's helping Dad to walk. And you know what? I think he's going to do it."

Looking at our father dripping with sweat, we were both amazed to see a glowing smile on his face. His dream of walking again might just become a reality.

"Hi, Dad," I cried out when he took a break. "I'm home."

Blowing out a puff of hot air, he announced with joy, "I'm going to walk again!"

Hugging his neck, I kissed his cheek and agreed. "I think you are."

Then, walking up to Junior, I shook his hand and gave him a hug around his expansive frame.

"I'm so pleased to meet you!"

"You must be Jackie," he said, hugging me back. "Your dad is one tough soldier. I've been working him hard these last couple of days."

Looking at the clock, I noticed it was past Junior's dismissal time. He was only hired for six hours with no overtime allowed.

"Oh Junior, you need to go. I don't want you in trouble for staying longer than commissioned."

"No worries. I clocked out an hour ago. I couldn't leave him. We were having so much fun."

Knowing this was divine intervention, I asked if he was available for a few more days. Happily, he had no other plans.

Later that night, it was time to have the talk with Dad as I finished preparing him for bed.

"So, what do you think about Junior?" I began, fluffing the pillows under his head.

"Oh, he's great. You know it's nice to have a man to talk to."

"I bet! How would you like to keep him?"

Pausing for a moment, a look of concern veiled his face. "What would happen to Enemi?"

"Well, I'll have to let her go. It makes me sad, but she's hurt herself, and I think she needs to rest. I'll let her keep all the money we paid for this month. She's only worked a week so far. The rest can be severance pay."

"How much is Junior?" Dad asked, a nervous infliction lacing his voice.

"A lot more, but you deserve the best."

Shaking his head, he let out a growl much like a wolf about to attack its prey. "No, I don't want to pay for it."

Frustration now pulling at the roots of my highlighted hair, I stopped for a moment to find just the right words.

"Dad, what are you saving all that money for?"

A pause suffocated the room.

"Dad?"

Looking away, he motioned me to leave.

"No, Dad! Why don't you want to pay for the care you deserve?"

"Because I want you kids to have it," I heard from his pillow.

Cupping his face in my hands, I turned his eyes in my direction.

"I don't want it! And the boys don't either. We want you to have a life that's comfortable and safe. Sometimes you have to pay for the best." Seeing a glimmer of understanding in his Irish eyes, I asked, "Wasn't your time better with Junior?"

Nodding, he added, "He even cooked dinner for us the two nights you were gone. And it was from scratch with healthy stuff."

"Really? Better than my cooking?" I smirked, knowing the answer had to be yes. "Well then, that seals the deal. I'll take care of everything."

Kissing him goodnight, I held him a little longer than usual. Maybe this was how I'd be able to do right by him. Maybe this would bring him some joy before his time on Earth was done.

The following morning, I called Lisa to set up a contract. Next, I called Enemi to give her the bad news. While it broke my heart, for she had become a part of the family, I knew that it would be best not only for my father, but her too. She just couldn't go on any longer.

For the next few months, Junior arrived not only on time, but early, and clocked out when required, but always stayed longer to be sure Dad was safely tucked away. The linens were washed, folded, and put away. My house was dusted and vacuumed. And every night I arrived home to a delicious meal waiting.

But the best part of our new arrangement was that Dad was diligently working on walking again. Jenny also came as usual, but more for moral support as Junior grabbed Dad out of his chair into a standing position. And, to everyone's astonishment, slowly his limbs began to move again.

"Jackie, when are you coming home today?" Junior asked one Wednesday morning as I was preparing for another day of uncertainty in real estate land. "Your dad has something to show you."

"What?"

"Can you come home for lunch? It's a surprise."

Loving surprises, especially when they involved my father, I rushed back at noon. Somehow, Lauren got the memo too, and together we witnessed Jack Madden walk again. Like a toddler making his first steps towards his parents, the room burst in excitement.

"Wow, Grandpa!" Lauren shrieked as she videotaped him take step after step toward the front door. "That's amazing."

With about five steps left to his target, Dad had to sit down. Tears of joy exploded down everyone's cheeks. I'd never seen him so proud.

Running to give him a hug, I cheered, "Dad, that was amazing!"

"I bet you thought I'd never be able to do it." He grinned. "Next time, I'll make it all the way."

Bending low so our eyes locked, I said with all certainty, "If there was ever anyone who could do this, it is you. I'm so happy for you."

CHAPTER 22

The Final Transition

"Jackie, the election is coming soon. I'm not registered to vote." We were nearing the end of September. With the 2012 presidential election a month away, his right to vote became a burning point on his checklist of things to do.

"What are you talking about? Of course you are."

"No! When you moved me here I became a resident of a different county. You can only vote in the county in which you live. I need to get an absentee ballot," he grumbled. "I've never missed an election in seventy-eight years. I'm not missing this one."

I knew he expected me to take care of this immediately, and my shoulders slumped. I had a list a mile long of things to do that day, but now they'd have to wait.

I had no idea how to get an absentee ballot and where to get the form, so I Googled it.

Opening a page with instructions on how to download the form, my fear of spending the day running around was immediately calmed.

"It takes two minutes to get your absentee ballot," I read. "Get started now."

Rushing back to let him know all was good, I found him

sound asleep, most likely from exhaustion over the worry of it all. It seemed that almost any amount of worry could cause fatigue to haunt his days. Just two weeks before, he was a proud man as he almost walked to the door. Now, just the mention of standing brought heaviness to his eyes.

"He seems even more tired than usual," I mentioned to Junior as he chopped the onions for Dad's stew. "We never talk anymore at night. Once he's in bed, he's out."

"Well, Jack is nearing ninety-seven. That's to be expected."

Taking a carrot that was about to be added to the pot, I began to chew on it, thinking of all the changes I'd witnessed lately.

"I'm just concerned. He seems to be worried about all kinds of things. Today he was in a state over getting an absentee ballot, yesterday he wanted to start organizing his taxes. For some reason, he feels there's not enough time."

"Not enough time? They're not due until April." Junior giggled. "But he's always been a man who wanted order in his life and things done in a timely manner. I would imagine voting is no different."

Even though I knew that, I still found it all a bit confusing. It would be several months before I even received any of the documents I needed to get his taxes ready.

"Do you think he's coming down with something?" I asked. "Maybe he's got a bug. You don't think he's developing dementia?"

Junior continued to stir the pan.

"The nurse was here yesterday and she said he's as healthy as an ox. So maybe he just has a lot on his mind."

For the next few days, things went the way they always did. His routine never faltered. It had been sixteen months since he moved in. I know if it had been me, I'd want to shake things up a bit, like maybe eat breakfast in bed before getting bathed, or watch a racy movie instead of saying prayers at the exact time every night. But my father liked his order, his routine, and knowing what was to happen at any given moment. As with Irish tradition of long ago, deviation was not allowed. But the one thing that did change was his conversation.

"I need to give Bill a call," Dad informed Junior the following Saturday morning. I was teaching my aerobics class at the YMCA, and Junior was getting him ready for the day.

"Who's Bill?" Junior asked, never hearing the name before.

"My brother. I have to call him. It's very important."

Knowing my dad was the last soldier standing in the Madden family, Junior became perplexed.

"Jack, is Bill older or younger than you?"

"He's my older brother."

Doing the math wasn't complicated. My father was ninety-six and the baby of three children. That would have made my uncle over one hundred.

"Jack, didn't your brother pass on?"

For a moment, my father's face went blank. Then, as if he realized he said something stupid, he shook his head and said, "Never mind."

Junior relayed the story to me when I arrived home an hour later.

"Why is he saying all this weird stuff lately?" I wondered aloud.

Junior shook his head. He was in the dark as much as I was. A little later, as I was about to jump into the shower, I heard a bellowing. "Jackie! Jackie!"

Running into the family room, I found him in his chair, waving his arms as if he were Donald Trump on "The Apprentice" and just about to fire someone.

"I need to get a contractor," he demanded as he rubbed his forehead vehemently. "I need to build the driveway so it slants up. It needs to get done soon."

Puzzled, I asked, "Whose driveway and what's the name of the contractor?"

"Mine of course. It needs the certain specifications for just the perfect angle."

Feeling not just confused but scared now, I was worried he was completely losing it.

"Dad, who is it you want me to call?"

"The contractor, you know. I want the slant to be specific."

I heaved a sigh. "I'm sorry. I don't know what contractor you're talking about."

And just like that, he shook his head, flit his hand for me to go away, and mumbled, "Never mind."

For the rest of the day and until the following morning, I lost him to that dark place he went when he was frightened, confused, or scared: sleep.

"Hi Dad," I called as I was preparing to leave the following day. "How are you doing today?"

Rubbing the sleep out of his eyes, he smiled.

"You off to work?"

"Yes, but I need to ask you something. Junior said you asked for Bill yesterday."

Shaking his head, I could tell he didn't want to talk about it.

"Remember, Bill's been gone for forty years."

With sorrow in his voice and a loneliness I hadn't heard since my mother passed away, he uttered, "How I miss him."

"I know you do. I bet you miss everyone. You know they're all waiting for you."

"Well, they can wait a little longer. I'm not ready," he grumbled, instantly losing the sentimental mood.

Kissing his forehead, I agreed. "Yes, Dad. You go when you're ready."

Later that night, I became increasingly concerned. He hadn't been with it for days now. It was almost as if he was in another space and time, but when called on it, he immediately snapped back into place, like the Fisher Price plastic beads my children once played with.

Hearing mumbling from down the hall, I looked at the clock: 2:00 a.m. Thinking he needed something, I got out of bed, but as I got closer I could hear he was having a conversation with someone.

Who in the hell could he be talking to?

Then I heard, "Lassie, Lassie . . ."

Standing at his bedroom door, I watched his hand reach for the window, stretching out as far as he could.

What does he see? There's nothing there. It was as if he was communicating with the other side, insistent that my mom be with him.

After several minutes, I interrupted the invisible reunion.

"Dad," I called. "Can I help you with something?"

Instantly, he pulled his arm back and switched gears.

"My watch doesn't work anymore. I think the battery is dead."

Coming to sit by his side, I gently took hold of his arm to have a look at the watch my mother had given him years ago—a Timex that, like him, took a licking, kept on ticking, and never seemed to run out of batteries. But now it had. Was my father running out of batteries too?

"I can get that fixed for you in the morning."

"I want you to get into bed with me."

Get into bed with him? Sorry, Dad, that feels creepy.

Pulling myself together, rather than ask a bunch of questions that might lead to nowhere, I simply said, "Dad, there's not enough room for me to lie down with you."

Patting the right side of the bed, the side my mother always slept on, he announced, "Yes there is. Right here."

As I walked around to the other side, my mind was spinning. What had happened to my father? Was he on some new medication that made him loopy? But seeing this was important to him, I positioned myself on the side Mom held for years, bent over the railing, and put my cheek to his.

"I can't get on the bed, but I'm right here."

"Ah, my sleepy-time girl."

That's what he used to call her when she'd fall asleep on the couch in the afternoon sun. He really thought I was Mom.

Afraid to burst his bubble or do some damage to his psyche, I kept my cheek on his for several minutes as we connected in silence. Just when I was about to kiss him goodnight, thinking he was now calm and ready for sleep, he started up again.

"Why didn't we have more babies? I wanted lots of children."

I'm definitely calling the social worker tomorrow. This is cuckoo.

Rather than correct him, I played along.

"Jack, we got married later. We were in our thirties when we had the first three and I was forty when Michael was born. My body was wearing out. I couldn't have more."

Letting out a sigh, he went on and on about how he loved children and how he had wanted a houseful.

Then, out of left field, he asked, "Have you stopped smoking?"

Remembering how my mother struggled before quitting in 1968, I stated with confidence, "Yes, I quit a long time ago."

"Good! That was a disgusting habit."

For the next couple of minutes, we talked about our children, or should I say their children. Wanting to be remembered in the best light, I began saying glowing things about their daughter.

"Jackie was always such a good girl, wasn't she?"

To my surprise, this time there was no mention of my being sneaky.

"Yes, Lassie. She still is."

But, just as strangely as the conversation began, it switched back, as if he were playing with a nightlight by his bed. One minute I was his wife, the next, I was his daughter again.

"Jackie, I think I can go to sleep now. Thanks for the chat."

The following morning, I gave Tracie a call. I was sitting in my car at the office, afraid to have this conversation around other people.

His behavior had been extremely bizarre the past week and I needed clarification on what was going on. Did all old people get confused? Had his medication changed? Was he going nuts? My father used to be present and alert. Was I losing him to some mental abyss?

As I relayed the episodes of the week, Tracie listened quietly. Then, with kindness in her voice, the kind you hear when about to receive bad news, she said, "Jackie, your dad's in his final transition. He's letting you know he's leaving."

"Leaving? Leaving where? What do you mean, like dying?"

Somewhere in my subconscious, I already knew this, but I didn't want to believe it. It was so much easier to blame his behavior on medication than the fact that our time together was now coming to an end. I put my head on the steering wheel and began to cry.

"How much time does he have?"

"What he's doing is what we call one foot in, one foot out. His spirit is preparing to leave and all that talk is his way of preparing you. But, in his reality, he doesn't know it. He'll say odd things, but when called on them, he will immediately jump back to the present."

Now sobbing uncontrollably, I sat with the phone to my ear, wanting once again to run and hide. All of a sudden, all those times when he drove me crazy and I wanted him gone were erased. I wanted it to be the first day he moved in. I wanted to be up late at night, exhausted but chatting about what was important to him: his thoughts, feelings, dreams, and fears. I wanted to be a little girl again, trotting behind him as he mowed the lawn. I wanted to see his head pop into my room at night to see if I needed any help with my homework. I wanted to hear him coo, "you'll be just fine" a million more times. I wanted time to stand still.

"Jackie, we never know how long this will take. It could be three weeks or three months," Tracie continued. "But, when he talks, play along. As long as he doesn't fall into a place that could be mentally damaging, just let him talk."

"But I don't want him to go. I'm not ready."

"I'll be right here if you need me. Call me any time. He's a remarkable man who's had an amazing life. And, most importantly, he's been loved, especially by you."

As I hung up, I stared out the window at the rain that was now falling. I knew this day would come, but I wasn't prepared for the reality of it. I wonder if we're ever truly prepared for the emptiness that replaces the space a loved one once filled.

Realizing how short my time was, I was also hit with the recognition that I wasn't the same woman I was when I took him in. My father had touched the most precious of all musical notes in my spiritual core bringing me back to what was true, honest, and real: God, prayer, and a heart filled with daily gratitude. He did this without pontification on what was right, but with his example of a life filled with grace and dignity. Oh, how I was going to miss him.

CHAPTER 23

A Time for Goodbye

For the next couple of weeks, Dad and I talked more when he was awake, but his foot was always trapped on the other side.

On October 10, as I fed him his dinner, he declared, "Jackie, I need my blue suit. I want it cleaned and pressed. And my favorite tie, the one I wore to your wedding."

That blue suit had sat in his closet for over thirty years and only saw the light of day for important religious events, such as Christmas, baptisms, or weddings. How I loved seeing him in it, his snow-white hair in perfect contrast to its navy color. My father was always, in my opinion, the most handsome man I'd ever known, and his blue suit put the stamp on the letter.

Remembering what Tracie said, I played along with the conversation.

"Okay, Dad," I answered, spooning mushy boiled chicken into his gaping mouth. "But why do you need it?"

"I'm going to get all dressed up, then I'm going for a drive."

"Where are you going? Can I come?" I found myself giggling.

"Junior is going to put me in the car and first we're going to drive to the living room, then I have to rest." He smiled, as if he were letting me in on some wonderful secret and whispered with his index finger covering his mouth. "Yes, we're going to drive to the living room, and when I'm ready, we're going out the door."

Noticing that he was now pointing his finger upward, my eyes suddenly stung with tears that would flow when I left the room. He was having visions of how his life would be at the end, and he wanted me to know all the details.

Bending over to kiss his forehead, I patted his cheek and reassured him I'd get it cleaned and ready.

A few weeks into Junior's appearance into our lives, we realized he'd need the weekends off. So, after several misses, another perfect solution stepped in. The dart that hit the bull's eye: Mike Toll.

Mike was a physically fit man in his forties. He'd had many careers over his lifetime but was thinking of becoming a nurse and felt working in the caregiving industry would give him insight into what that career would be like. While Junior spoke to Dad's heart, Mike touched my soul with his deep spiritual nature.

"I bet you have a lot of thoughts running through you now," Mike said when he found me teary eyed and staring at the birds flying around the feeder outside.

"I'm scared," I uttered, not wanting to look at him. My tears were constant now, and no amount of cold water would reduce the puffiness around my eyes. "I'm afraid I'll miss something, but I'm so tired."

"I'm here with you. I won't let you miss anything."

For so many months, I'd been angry. I was pissed that Enemi was in the house all the time, even though she was a sweet woman. I found it creepy to come home, so I'd spend time in the neighborhood park or eating frozen yogurt in my car just killing time because I didn't want to face it all.

I was annoyed that my brothers were so far away, that my friends rarely called anymore to see how I was doing, and I was especially irritated that my body had become lumpy with the lack of exercise it was once used to. While my father was dying, in so many ways I felt I was the one who died long ago. But now we were near the end, all those feelings of angst and betrayal were gone. I saw them for what they truly were—the feelings of a woman on overload spinning in a vortex of pain, guilt, and shame over her own personal feelings that she was projecting on others.

For the next week and a half, the visits from Hospice became more frequent to check his vital signs. He was still eating as usual, drinking plenty of fluids, and his body was functioning as it always did—plenty of full diapers.

"He's just fine," Mary announced each time she left. "I see no signs of any true decline. His temperature is normal, there is no discoloration in his fingertips, and his mind is still very with it. He even asked me who I was voting for."

With a smile and a wink, she grabbed her amulet that always hung around her neck and giggled. "Of course, I told him the Democrats. I didn't want him to have a heart attack."

It was now October 18. His absentee ballot had arrived and we had work to do.

"Okay, Dad. Are you ready to vote?" I asked as he rested in bed. He was spending more time in his room these days. It seemed a much more comfortable place for him to meditate on his life.

At his nod, I opened the ballot, took out my black pen, and jokingly asked, "Who do you want to vote for?"

Without any hesitation, he proudly announced, "Everyone and everything Democratic!"

Drawing the black lines from the candidate's name to their party, it took no time at all.

"Do you think Obama has a chance?" I asked, knowing he'd say, "He better."

In 2008, Barack Obama was about to inherit the biggest mess this country had seen since the Great Depression. Unemployment was at 10 percent and millions of citizens were uninsured, using the emergency rooms in hospitals as their way to receive care. The housing market had tanked and everywhere you looked, people were discouraged about the future.

"I hope he does," he answered, pointing to his glass of water. Talking politics always made him thirsty. "No president could do anything in one term with the nightmare we've been living in. Sadly, I think he needs three terms to make anything good come out of it."

As I handed him the water, I found myself wondering what it must be like to have lived for almost ninety-seven years. Dad was born in 1916. World War I was in full swing, the president was Woodrow Wilson, and the League of Nations would soon be created. The average price of a home was $5,000, a car a mere $400, and postage stamps were only 2 cents apiece.

Thinking this would be a fun conversation, I asked, "Dad, what's it like to be almost ninety-seven?"

Looking at me as if this was the stupidest question he'd ever heard, and that I'd left my mind someplace, he answered, "I have no idea."

"No, Dad! Think about it. You've seen so many inventions over the years, so much history has unfolded, and new ways of thinking are the norm. What does that feel like?"

Seeing his daughter was serious, he put his arm behind his head and looked out the window. The birds he loved were getting ready for the winter again, just as he was preparing for his winter.

"I still have no idea because in my mind, I'm sixteen."

"But don't you ever get upset about how your body changed with time?"

Turning towards me, his eyes narrowed as if I were about to get schooled big time. "That's a woman thing!"

A woman thing? I wanted to yell. But he was right. I was conditioned by my grandmother and mother to never leave home without my face on, hair curled, and body wrapped in a pretty dress. Vanity was definitely my middle name.

"Really? I wish I could be like that."

Covering him up, I put his headphones on and turned on channel 229. It was time I reevaluated my own aging process. I always got emotional over a wrinkle that wasn't there the day before, a new vein that seemed to pop out on my leg just for walking to the kitchen, and the dulling hue of my once shiny blonde curls. To me, the aging process sucked because it meant I was growing old and would become undesirable. But for him, it didn't matter what age he was. He was just happy to be alive.

On the following weekend, we spent time talking about the Giants and whether they could possibly win another World Series. They'd taken the title just two years before in 2010 and it seemed nearly crazy for them to pull it off again. Dad also became increasingly concerned that his checks were going to all the right accounts. His biggest worry was that his beloved Giants were paid on time.

"Make sure they get their money," he instructed, agitated, as the catcher, Buster Posey, made a home run.

"How am I going to do that?"

"Call them, and if they say they haven't received their paychecks, pay them for me."

"Out of your accounts?" I laughed, thinking he must love them more than his own kids.

Realizing he was talking silly, he became present, grabbed my arm and pulled me close.

"I love you, honey."

Patting his cheek, I replied in kind, "And I love you."

Since his health seemed to be okay, I decided to spend a little time in the office the following Monday. I'd been gone for two weeks. If nothing else, I was sure I had some bills that needed attention.

But, as usual, I came home at noon only to find him still in bed.

"Aren't you getting up today?" I asked, bringing in his mail.

"No, I just want to stay here today. How did it go at work? Any new listings?"

Gently tracing the lines that traversed his wrinkled cheek, I leaned in for my kiss.

"No, not today. I'm having a hard time this year. Real estate is like that, you know."

As we sat and talked about the challenges of the market, he questioned me on my strategy, gave suggestions on where to find some clients, and ended the conversation as he always did: "Honey, don't you worry. You'll be just fine."

I'd heard him say that simple phrase my entire life and had so grown to love hearing it. They were just four little words, but they were strung together with the finest gold thread that tied his heart to mine. My father always had the utmost faith in me. Maybe it was time I did too.

Just as I was about to ask him if he wanted anything to eat, I noticed his eyes moving back and forth on the wall behind me. Turning around, I saw nothing unusual. There were no bugs on the march, the picture of the forest wasn't crooked, and there was no one behind me. Then he asked, "Who is that woman?"

"What woman?"

Indicating with his hand that he wanted me to move so he could get a better look, he stared steadily at the wall as I got up and went to the other side of the bed and put my cheek on his.

"What does she look like?" I whispered.

"She's beautiful and so nice. She looks like your mother."

He continued looking at the vision of my mother while I stared at the wall.

Then I said, "It is Mom. She misses you. But, remember, you go when you're ready."

And just like that, she was gone and he was asleep.

For the next couple of days, he mostly slept. The nurses came daily, but there were no physical signs he was leaving—that is, until Thursday, when I had someplace else to be.

Michelle had been living in Los Angeles pursuing her acting career. She was filming a movie in New Orleans and was having a bed delivered that Friday. It was a gift from a friend who was cleaning out her storage locker, and Friday was the only day it could be brought to her home. We'd made the decision the month before that I'd come down and have a mini vacation in her apartment and receive it. At that time, all was well at home. I'd leave on Thursday and be back Sunday night. Arrangements were made with David and Tim to tag team and stay with our father. Since we hired Junior and Mike, I was completely covered.

I didn't really need my brothers to come, but something inside me suggested this would be a good time for them to visit.

On Thursday morning, I entered Dad's room to let him know I'd be leaving soon. We'd discussed it many times over the past several weeks and he'd always been happy to know I was going to be able to get away. Today was different.

Hearing I was about to leave, he suddenly became frightened. Shifting his body weight from side to side, he tried to pull himself upwards, then, made retching sounds as if he were about to throw up.

"Oh my God, Dad! Are you okay?"

Grabbing a nearby bowl, he proceeded to lose the bile in his stomach. With scared, pleading eyes, he begged, "Please, don't go!"

It was in that moment I knew he didn't have much time left. Tracie had warned me of the signs when it came close to the end: fear, agitation, body discoloration, and loss of appetite. But I also remembered her saying, "He won't leave unless you're in the room with him. You two have made this incredible journey together and he'll want you with him."

Knowing he'd be with two of his sons, I made the difficult decision to go.

"Dad, once you're settled, I'm going to go. I promised Michelle I'd do this for her. But I'll come home Saturday morning instead of Sunday night. David will be here in a couple of hours and Tim comes tomorrow night. Even Michael said he'd be here when I get back. We'll have a party!"

Four hours later, I was on a plane to Los Angeles, preparing myself for a life without my father.

What will I do without him? I thought as my eyes watered.

I thought I'd be ready when the time came, but I'm not. The next day, I received my daughter's bed, then sat on the Santa Monica beach and sobbed for hours.

On Saturday morning when I returned, Mike, David, and Tim were trying to change his diaper. His body had become such dead weight it now took three strong men to move him. As they rolled him over, I touched his shoulder. "Dad, I'm home." Grabbing my arm, he cried, "I don't want to do this anymore. I want to go back."

Wrapping him in my arms, I nuzzled my nose in his neck and whispered, "Okay, Dad. Okay."

For the next thirty-eight hours, my brothers and I sat at his side. We talked, told stories just like we had when we were by my mother's side, and held his hand. By 1:00 p.m. Sunday, David needed to leave. He had classes to teach early the next day at Sacramento State, but he planned to return in two days.

"What is that sound?" Tim asked Mike. Dad was making a gurgling noise in his throat. "It sounds like he's got fluid in there but can't cough it up."

"They call it the death rattle," he confirmed. "Saliva and other secretions accumulate in the upper chest, but he doesn't have the strength to clear them out."

Dad lay quiet, as if in a deep sleep, his breathing shallow. The only noise in the room was the rise and fall of the gurgling sound each time he labored for air.

"Jackie, I think we need to get hospice involved. I'm going to call them and let them know what's happening," Mike informed me.

Nodding, I sat down and held my father's hand. In my heart, I knew it was only a matter of hours.

For the next five hours, hospice was on the phone every half hour, instructing Mike what to do next. Being that I was the main caregiver, it was up to me to administer the morphine, droplet by droplet.

Tearing the top off the tiny plastic vial, I kissed his cheek, then inserted the tube deep inside his mouth and squeezed the contents.

"How are you doing?" Mike asked at about 3:00 p.m. I hadn't left Dad's side the entire day.

Smiling, I looked into his compassionate eyes and grabbed his hand for comfort.

"I'm okay, I guess. It's so surreal. All this felt like it would take forever, and now it's here."

By 4:30 p.m., our wonderful caregiver started preparing to leave. There was laundry to fold, the logbook to write the day's notes in, the phone call to make that he was signing out, and one last vial of morphine. Cutting off the tip, he handed me the tube.

"He's stopped rattling," I said as I squeezed the last dose in. "Thank you for being with me today."

Patting my shoulder, he said goodbye and turned to collect his things.

"Tim, aren't the Giants about to play?" I asked, desperately needing a diversion.

"Yeah, if they win tonight they take the World Series."

"Let's get the headphones and put the game on. Dad can still hear. They say hearing becomes acute at the end. Let's let him listen to his last game."

Forty-five minutes later, the first run for the Giants came racing across home plate. With the audio going directly into the headphones, Tim planted himself close to the screen to watch in silence.

Just then, I heard a voice deep within say, "Talk to him."

Talk to him? What am I supposed to say?

"Just talk to him."

I wasn't sure what I was supposed to be saying, but taking off his headphones, I wrapped him up like an infant, holding him close to my chest. Magically, the words poured out. It was time to let him go.

"Dad, you don't have to do this anymore. I know you've stayed here as long as you have because you've been worried about me," I began, whispering in his ear. "I love you, I will miss you, but I'll be just fine."

With a final puff of air in his lungs, he let go and his energy took its wings and flew with a rush back to his family, my mother, and his friends. Back to the source that had guided him his entire life to always be an instrument of peace. He was gone and I was now a girl without a father.

"Dad just left," I cried to Tim.

Turning away from the TV, my brother stared.

"No, he didn't."

"Yes, he did. I gave him permission to go and he took it," I wept. "I didn't really mean it. Why would he listen to me now? He never did before. I want him back."

As I crumbled into a puddle of tears, Tim came to my side and held me. Together we sat in silence with the body of the man we called father, but whose soul's journey on earth was now complete.

CHAPTER 24

The First Hundred Days

For the next week, I wandered aimlessly from one room to another, lost and confused. I shouldn't have been surprised. After all, I'd spent fifteen years deep in the trenches of caregiving for both my parents. I was now a career soldier without a war to fight.

Lying in my bed at night, I found myself thinking back to the days when our family was whole: four Madden kids bound by rules and expectations so they'd be on the right path for a positive future, but always surrounded with pure love. Our parents prepared us for everything that would come our way and provided us with the methods to succeed: how to get into good colleges, what jobs we should seek for financial security, tips for parenting our own children, and how to pray when life became challenging. But the one thing they never prepared us for was how to live in a world without them.

"How are you doing?" I was asked repeatedly as friends called to check in on me.

Knowing they were just trying to be kind, I developed a script, something easy that would roll off the tongue and not cause me to burst into tears.

"Okay."

But if I were truly honest, I was devoid of feeling anything at all. It was as if a piece of me died along with him and all that was left was a dull numbness. I was now a sixty-year-old orphan with no direction.

There's been a lot written about the loss of the second parent. Instantly, your own mortality starts tapping at the door, whispering, "You're next." You realize the people who loved you the longest, even before you were born, are gone forever and that no one will ever love you the same again.

There'd be no more Christmas or birthday presents from Mom and Dad, no more phone calls just to say "hi." Gone were the days where I believed I could do anything just because my father and mother told me I could.

But the most troubling thing of all was realizing there'd be a rumbling shift in the tectonic plates that once held my brothers and I together on the same plane.

Without our parents acting as the tools in the needlework of the cable knit blanket that once enfolded our family, keeping us safe and protected, the missing yarn would soon cause their life's masterpiece to unravel.

For over thirty years, my brothers came home because Mom and Dad were alive. Now that they were gone, there'd be no reason for them to come back. No longer would I see them at the holidays. I worried our connection would fade. They were free to focus on their lives with their families and I found myself crying that once again I no longer fit in. Other families fell apart when the last parent died. Why not mine too?

At first, people were kind, as they always are when someone experiences a loss. Cards flooded the mailbox with prayers and best wishes. How I wanted to read all the lovely things to Dad just like when I came home for lunch. He would have loved all the niceties.

"Your father was a remarkable man."

"What a fabulous sense of humor he had with that dry wit of his."

"His will to live was beyond reproach."

On and on it went.

He would have also been proud to know people thought I was a good daughter. After all, he raised me as such. But as the accolades came pouring in, I found myself wishing they'd all just go away and leave me alone. I needed to process what had happened and how I would move forward without him. Going back to work would be the first step.

"Jackie, it's now your time. You are free!" a colleague stated as she threw her arms around me my first day back. "Life is now all about you."

Free? What the hell does that even mean? I thought. *For over half my life all I've done is take care of people: my children, then my parents. I don't even know who I am without someone to watch over.*

As the first couple of weeks trickled by, I spent my days glassy-eyed and weepy. At first, I cried over his loss, but then I began to become emotionally unglued with worry. Did I tell him enough how much I loved him? Did I ever tell my mom? When someone's gone permanently, we no longer have an opportunity to make amends for any digressions.

"I know I loved them both with every breath I took, but did I tell them enough?" I whimpered on the phone to Jenni. "Did I let them know what wonderful parents they were and that from the moment I was born the one thing I never doubted was that they loved me?"

Hearing her mother's regret, Jenni lovingly stated, "Mom, sometimes telling someone you love them has nothing to do with words. It's all in how they're treated, and you were there for them every step of the way. Please, don't regret any-thing."

"I know you're right. But I just can't seem to shake it. The house is so empty now."

I once heard loneliness described as fear, a feeling of help-lessness about where to turn next. I remembered feeling that way when my husband left. I was the mother of four teenagers, and that was not only isolating, but scary. Teenagers have a way of playing whiplash with a parent's heart. One minute they want and need you, the next you're dirt under their feet as they walk out the door to do God-knows-what with who-knows-who.

Along with the Tilt-A-Whirl we rode together, teenagers were very expensive. I'd had no idea how I'd keep their finances and lives going with private schools and a big house, despite the fact Dave honored his legal financial obligations. I felt that just because their parents couldn't fix their broken marriage, they shouldn't suffer, so overcompensating and enabling became the mission of every day.

But this fear was different.

"I just hurt so badly." I began to cry. "It's like someone has taken my Cutco knives and tested each blade out on my stomach. I wasn't prepared for this."

I grabbed the box of tissues as my child let me simmer down.

"It's funny. I don't even recognize my face when I look in the mirror. I look so old."

With a heavy sigh on the other end of the phone, Jenni searched to find just the right words to try and stop the bleeding in my wounded heart.

"Mom, we all look old when we're tired. Once you start

getting some rest, you'll feel better. Are you still taking the Ambien?"

"Yes, the doctor said I should just continue to take it so I can sleep for a couple more months. Then she wants me to wean myself."

"Well, do what she says. At least you can turn off the voices in your head at night."

So, it was. I drugged myself at night to sleep and walked around like a zombie during the day. The one thing I could count on was my children's concern for their fragile mom.

"How are you doing?" Lauren asked on her way to work the following week. We were nearing our first Thanksgiving without Dad and without my brothers. Our family would celebrate with just four women in our home. Even Timmy was gone, now living in Spain.

"I'm good," I lied. "It's so weird. I find myself just listening to the quiet. There's no more channel 229, no more heavy breathing while he napped, and no calls for me in the middle of the night to chat. It's all so strange."

"Mom, remember how you complained how quiet it was because he slept all the time? Maybe you should think of this as listening to peace."

How right she was. Peace is a different kind of silence. Peace is when you live in the moment with no concern for what will be or how it will affect you. I needed to learn how to live like that.

"Yes, that's a good way to look at it. But even Maddie isn't barking. I think she's missing him terribly. I find her lying under his bed as if she's wondering where he went." Our now eleven-year-old pound puppy had attached herself to my father, and had stayed with him wherever he was

"They were so cute together," Lauren reminisced. "You know, Grandpa would always ask if she were close by when I visited. It's funny how he grew to love her."

"Yes, it was so sweet. She'd sleep in his room until about 1:00 in the morning, then come to her bed in my room," I remembered. "In some ways, I think it's harder on her than me. At least I understand it all."

Just as I was saying goodbye, Maddie found her way to my side and put her head in my lap. Patting her long, golden torso, a wave of grief so palatable I could taste the bitterness in my mouth came over me. For ten years I'd done a lot of crying. I mourned the loss of my marriage, became sad over the depressed woman my mother had become at the end, and shed tears as I waved goodbye to my life's only purpose, my children, as they left for lives of their own.

But the guttural heaving sobs that now spewed forth were coming from the deepest of all cavities. My life's anchor had been unmoored from the seabed, and I became a tiny wrecked vessel floating aimlessly in the ocean with no beacon to show me the way. This was not going to be an easy process.

Thanksgiving came and went with no fanfare, no humongous meal, and no extra guests. We had decided to honor Dad's life on December 20. His grandchildren would all be able to attend, and it would be as Dad would have liked, with those he loved praying in church together.

In our early discussions about how he wanted to die, he made the decision to be cremated.

"I don't want you kids spending a lot of money on a coffin," he stated one evening during a late-night chat. "You can just burn the remains and bury the ashes in the family plot."

"Really, Dad? I'm surprised you would say that. Are you sure you don't want to bury your body? That's what you used to want."

Taking his bed sheet and pulling it up to his chin, I wondered if he were trying to hide from the discussion. Then, peering those Irish blue eyes over the top, he shook his head. "Oh God, no! The idea of bugs crawling all over my body gives me the willies."

The plans were made. The church was contacted, scriptures selected, and music planned. The mortuary took care of his remains. It was the same mortuary that took care of my mother, another of his final wishes. When I went to pick up his ashes, a precisely folded American flag was laid in my hands.

"We want to thank your father for all the years of service he gave this country," the woman from behind the counter said. "I'm sure he was a remarkable man."

Smiling as the tears streamed, I was never so proud of my father than in that moment. Like all men of that time, my father served, but he never saw action. Having a brilliant mathematical mind, the Navy felt his talents were better served in the Supply Corps. This bothered him for years, feeling he added nothing to the victory. We spent many nights in my house with me trying to convince him that without his service, those men overseas would not have received their paychecks or the supplies desperately needed to carry out their missions. His contribution to the war effort had been terribly important.

"Thank you," I answered, grabbing for a tissue in my purse. "Yes, my father was a remarkable man."

I once heard that while we have a birthdate and a death date on our tombstone, it's the hyphen in the middle that says it all, for it's the story of our lives. Accepting the box in the blue velvet bag, I thought of how my father had punctuated all our lives. The trajectory of my life would forever change because of his example. I would strive to live a life of gratitude, prayer, and hope.

It was a gray day when we celebrated his life on an inconvenient day on the calendar so close to Christmas, yet, the room had a nice representation of friends to celebrate his life with us, not too big, not too small. Just the way he would have liked it. He never wanted a fuss.

I sat smiling as I soaked in the experience. The pain of his loss was fading some and I'd stopped crying every day. As the music played, I looked at his eight grandchildren. Timmy, who was now living abroad, had come home from Spain as a surprise and I was thrilled to see all the children together. There were also Dad's four children, two daughters-in-law, even his former son-in-law, Dave, and I couldn't help but be proud. My father was loved.

My brother David patted my shoulder.

"It's perfect, Jackie," he whispered. "Dad would have loved this."

"Yes, it is perfect, isn't it? And, now he can truly rest in peace."

EPILOGUE

Time to Move On

Shortly after my father's passing, my promise to Jenni was fulfilled as well: her room was restored to a pretty, feminine, and diaper-free space.

Tim and I decided to clear out everything in Dad's room—all his clothes, shoes, toiletries, walker, and hospital bed—within hours of his passing. By the end of the day, it was as if he'd never lived there, except for the stains on the floor and the bruised and battered furniture and walls from his misguided wheelchair. Just like my childhood room the day I emptied it to prepare our family home for market, the space looked naked. Soon after, I painted the walls a more subdued shade of yellow, fresh carpet was laid, and new blue, green, and white linens adorned her bed. The soft colors reminded me of springtime, and despite the fact Jenni once feared her grandfather would die in her private space, it now became a place of joy, not only for her but for all of us, for he was allowed a peaceful death in a loving environment. The end of his life had been everything I prayed it would be, and I could move on knowing I did my best.

By 2014, life was beginning to feel somewhat normal again. Dad had been gone two years, and I was back working more regularly. David and I had settled his living trust and divided the assets between his four children as Dad requested. I was learning to explore life again, taking an art class, new exercise classes, and getting together with long-lost friends. While the pain of his absence was still fresh in my heart, I was pleased time was doing her magic and healing the emptiness. It was also teaching me to not only learn to be grateful for our experience together, but to treasure it. If I hadn't taken on the job, I would have missed so much—like who my father truly was and who I was born to be.

On February 11 (the day that would have been his ninety-eighth birthday), I was looking through Jenni's closet for a coat she'd asked me to send her. Opening the doors, I found myself marveling at how quickly she had made her presence known again in this house. She'd been living in San Diego for eight years, but somehow, just like the stuff in my parents' home after the fire, her excess wardrobe had found its way back.

"Really Jenni!" I giggled to myself. "You haven't worn these things since college. Maybe it's time to purge."

Pushing aside seven dresses and five pairs of slacks, I found my way to three coats. Pulling out the one she wanted, I noticed my father's blue suit.

"I forgot about you," I heard myself saying, as if I'd just discovered a long-lost friend.

Pulling it out, I began to tear up. This wasn't just some piece of outdated men's apparel. It was a symbol of who my dad was: dignified, dependable, trustworthy, a man who respected himself and others. Every time he wore it, I thought, He's the handsomest man in the world.

Taking the jacket off the hanger, I put my arms into the

sleeves and wrapped them around my waist, remembering how he hugged me in it on my wedding day.

We were in the waiting room. Mom had just put the finishing touches on the flowers in my veil. Dad and I stood alone as panic seeped through every vein in my quivering body. By the look on my face, he knew I was having second thoughts.

"Are you okay?" he asked, putting his hand to my face.

"I don't know," I answered, a tear now escaping down my freshly made-up cheeks. My life was about to drastically change. Not only was I taking on another man's name, a name that for some was hard to pronounce, but we'd be moving to San Diego, 483 miles away. "What will I do without you nearby every day?"

He gently pushed the tear aside with his index finger and enfolded me in his arms. Silently, we held each other until we heard the church coordinator say, "It's time."

Releasing me from his loving grip, he looked deep into my eyes and said, "You'll be just fine."

Then, with a kiss, he led me down the aisle to give me away. Little did I know, he was holding back his own tears.

Standing before the mirror thirty-four years later, I stared at the image of an aging woman drowning in a blue jacket.

"Dad, I want you back," I sobbed as I clung to the coat. Putting my nose into the fabric, I could still smell him. "I lied when I told you I'd be just fine. Nothing is the same without you.

"I want to be little and sit in your lap again. I want to dance with you one more time. I want you to hold my hand and tell me over and over that you love me." I wept uncontrollably, covering my eyes with the long sleeves. "No one will ever love me the way you did."

When I was a little girl, I spent much of my solitary time in fantasyland, making up stories in my head of the man who would one day love me, marry me, and have a passel of children with me. We'd also live happily ever after.

When my marriage failed, I began searching for my true love, only to be constantly disappointed. Dating in your fifties is not like it is in your twenties. It felt like all the good ones were still married.

Studying the image before me, I mourned the lack of a relationship in my life. This was not how I was supposed to turn out. I knew all sorts of shitty things would happen, but the one thing I never considered was becoming a single woman.

Crying over the unfairness of it all, again I studied my reflection swaddled in the image of my dad and suddenly had an epiphany.

"I've been so stupid," I said aloud. "The love I was looking for . . . I had it all along."

What I hadn't seen was that what I had wanted was a soulful love that didn't just shine in present time but was eternal. I had this with my father. From the moment I was born, we connected on a spiritual plane that went beyond the physical connection to a metaphysical truth, where hearts and souls rise above egos.

Wiping the tears that now soaked not only my cheeks but the sleeves of his jacket, I began to smile. I would be just fine because I was given the gift of truly knowing unconditional love. I needed to move on. It's what he'd want. It's what he'd prepared me for.

Taking off the jacket, I carefully folded it and laid it on the bed next to his pants.

"It's time I gave you away," I said, smoothing out the

wrinkles. "You belong in the hands of another wonderful father so that they too can one day walk their daughter down the aisle."

The suit was about to have a rebirth, just like me.

While like my mother, I never wanted to throw out anything that had a memory attached to it, I realized I no longer needed the suit to remind me of my sweet father. The memory of him would be forever inscribed on my heart with indelible gold ink, just like that promise I'd made so many years before.

If I ever missed the sound of his voice, all I had to do to bring him near was close my eyes and remember those two strong hands that held mine from the day I was born until he left this world. The final circle of life was complete and I would be "just fine."

About the Author

Jackie Madden Haugh calls herself the Guardian of Memories, a storyteller who preserves family history in the written form. Her first book, *My Life in a Tutu*, the story of a single woman in her fifties searching for the woman she was born to be after divorce, was launched in 2015. She is a columnist for a local newspaper, *The Los Altos Town Crier*, where she writes  musings on how she sees the world. Jackie was born and raised in the Bay Area of northern California and is the mother of four adult children.